How to Write a Successful Business Plan

How to Write a Successful Business Plan

Julie K. Brooks
Barry A. Stevens

American Management Association

Library of Congress Cataloging-in-Publication Data

Brooks, Julie K.
    How to write a successful business plan.

    Bibliography: p.
    Includes index.
    1. Planning. 2. Corporate planning. 3. Communication
in management. I. Stevens, Barry A. II. Title.
HD30.28.B775   1987   658.4'012   86-22355
ISBN 0-8144-5873-4

Printing number

10 9 8 7 6 5 4 3 2

Preface

There are many people who gave their time and knowledge to help us during the preparation of this book. We would like to say thank you to each of them, in no particular order, in this section.

Richard M. White, Jr., kindly gave us permission to abstract material from his book, *The Entrepreneur's Manual.* This is particularly evident in the discussions of founder's stock systems, interactive testing, and marketing.

Dave Hirschberg and Gerald Feigen of the Small Business Administration provided small business statistics for us.

Dr. Marshall Burak, Dean of the School of Business at San Jose State University, arranged for permission to use the EXUS business plan as our sample, and provided interview comments used in several places in the book. Dr. John Baird of the School of Business—Graduate Programs, San Jose State University, aided us by arranging for several graduate classes to complete our questionnaires.

Deloitte, Haskins & Sells gave us permission to reprint an excellent discussion on valuation of a company from its handbook, *Raising Venture Capital: An Entrepreneur's Guidebook.*

Several company founders agreed to lengthy telephone interviews in spite of their busy schedules, including Norman G. Woolcott, Jr., President of Nor-Cote Chemical Company; Daniel A. Hosage, President of Davox Corporation; Gary N. Hughes, President of Precision Image Corporation; William H. Keller, President of Keller High Tech, Limited; A. Keith Plant, President of Speech Plus, Incorporated; Sam Occhipinti, Chief Financial Officer for Summa Four Corporation; D. C. Brandvold, President of Branchemco, Inc.; and W. J. (Jim) Hindman, President of Jiffy Lube International, Inc.

A. Keith Plant also gave us permission to use his firm's business plan as another sample in our text (see Appendix B).

Several principals and associates from venture capital firms also volunteered for lengthy telephone interviews. These individuals include Larry Mohr, General Partner of Mohr Davidow Ventures; Pat Hamner, Investment Associate with Capital Southwest Corporation; and Nick Stanfield, a Principal with MSI Capital Corporation.

John L. Kearney, a practicing attorney in Solana Beach, California, provided us with materials describing limited partnerships.

We should say thank you to over a hundred people who took the time to respond to our lengthy questionnaires sent to funders, founders, and graduate students.

Roberta Marx helped with the early stages of this book. Karl Weber of AMACOM Books made a significant contribution to the final form of this material. William Gladstone of Waterside Productions saw the opportunity for this work. Robert and Mary Jack Brooks provided a restful setting on Florida's Imperial Coast for the authors for a few brief but necessary days during preparation of the manuscript.

Contents

Introduction

There's got to be a pony in there somewhere.

This book is for people who have a dream. It's for people who work for themselves, or want to. It's for people who work for someone else and want to contribute to their companies' success. It's for people who own or manage an existing business and want to make it grow. It's for people who have an idea and are convinced, in spite of all the odds, that it can and will succeed. It's for people who refuse to give up their dreams.

Why This Book Was Written

Many materials on writing business plans are already available. Each of the large public accounting firms distributes a free outline and descriptive text on how a plan should be constructed. There are textbooks, college classes, and seminars on the subject. There are even authors of computer programs who offer seminars on how to use their software to produce winning business plans.

What makes this book different? The answer lies in the *approach*. Almost all of the literature on this topic relates only to creating business plans for presentation to professional investors—that is, to venture capital firms, to stock underwriters or small business investment companies, or to professional lenders such as banks. This is an important purpose for preparing a business plan, but not the only one.

Our approach is broader. The business plan is a powerful document that can help you succeed, even if your audience consists only of you and others inside your firm. However, there are many potential audiences, and each of them can help you in some way to achieve your goals while you in turn can help them. Some audiences may reject your plan and decline to help. Others may see an opportunity for mutual benefit and provide the help you need.

When writing the plan you can clearly define several kinds of help you can use and then select appropriate audiences that will benefit from giving you that help. By tailoring your plan to meet the needs of these audiences, you can improve your chances of getting what you are asking for. That's what this book is all about: Finding someone who will say "yes," doing your homework, and achieving a positive result.

In most books, a business plan is defined by implication as "a document you prepare when seeking funding." A successful plan is one that gets the funding you need.

In the approach we follow in this book, the terms "business plan" and "success" have expanded meanings:

A *business plan* is a process you undertake to help make your company grow, to increase profits, or to develop and market a product idea or service. One important result of this process is a document that describes how you plan to achieve specific business objectives and milestones.

A business plan is a *success* if you achieve the objectives and milestones you have defined in the plan.

Why have we broadened these definitions? Because a much broader range of activities is now included in the business planning process. For instance, deals can be made to share equipment and facilities, thereby allowing product development to proceed in advance of funding. Other kinds of deals can be made with customers and suppliers, thereby reducing the need for funding. Weaknesses in your firm or product can be corrected, allowing another try at securing funding.

If one of your objectives is to obtain funding, then so be it. Write it into the plan, and achieve it. If, however, like many people who seek funding, you are rejected, you can define an alternative path to your goals. For example, you may discover, as have a number of firms, that you can develop your product or firm to a point at which you no longer require outside funding.

By following the business planning process we describe, you can define alternative approaches that will take your firm or your product where you want it to go.

The Need for Professional Legal and Accounting Advice

The many suggestions and approaches presented in this book are the result of research and interviews with people involved in a wide cross section of small businesses. Some of the methods discussed may have significant legal and tax consequences, and firms or individuals should use discretion in their application. Neither the authors nor the publisher can make any guarantee regarding the suitability or effectiveness of any of the methods for your audience, for your firm, or for you. None of the material in this book is intended to replace competent, professional legal, accounting, and tax advice.

The Process Is the Key

Our emphasis, then, is on the entire sequence of events—from the inception of an idea to the presentation of a business plan as a process that can be learned and that can provide guidance and support when you encounter roadblocks and rejection. This process can be followed over and over again until some measure of success is attained.

A cynic would say that if the business plan is rejected, there's probably a good reason! That may be so. But we've observed many cases in which business plans reflecting perfectly good business opportunities, with a reasonable management team and the promise of an ample return on the original investment, were rejected.

People who want to succeed with product development, or who want to make their firms grow, should expect many rejections. They should get into the habit of responding to these disappointments by making any necessary improvements in their teams, approaches, services, or products, and then continuing their search for the kind of assistance they require.

There Is Plenty of Help Out There If You Want to Invent the Silicon Chip

As we prepared this book, we talked with many people who either were or are involved with the business planning process. Many had ideas and were trying to get financial support to implement them while others had managed to get started with their own firms. We spoke with venture capitalists, private investors, partners in accounting firms, lawyers, and bankers. One conclusion we reached was that, at any point in time, some topics and fields are viewed as "hot" by the venture capital community.

If your plan does not deal with a hot topic, you may not be able to stir up much interest in it.

The hot topics shift rapidly. While this book was in preparation, we received a series of reports that said venture capital firms had:

Sworn off software
Gone into mergers
Gone into medicine and genetics
Gone overseas
Gone into artificial intelligence software

From our viewpoint, what is considered *hot* emerges from a combination of technology that captures the attention of the investment community and the prospect of a significantly above-average return on investing in that technology. Many of the venture capital firms we contacted anticipate that only a few of their investments will really pay off, and that they rely on these investments that succeed to pay for the ones that fail.

From the perspective of the investment firms, a hot opportunity is one that shows a potential for a three-to-five-times return on the original investment. Averaged out over a long period of time, total profit margins for the professional investors could range between 20 and 40 percent.

The bad news then is that if your product idea or service is not hot, you may not be able to get an investor's attention. The good news is that you may have only to wait for your product idea or service to become hot again. In the meantime, you can develop alternative strategies to keep going.

Dealing with the Professional Financial Community

If you have had any dealings with the professional financial community, you know how difficult and demanding it can be. Venture capital firms want an assurance of a return that is significantly above average. Very few existing firms, and even fewer startup ones, can succeed with a stock offering. Small business investment companies force you to contend with a mountain of paperwork. Banks want you to play "you bet your house," maximizing your risk and minimizing theirs. Finally, an overwhelming percentage of business plans sent to all of these professional investors are rejected, many without a detailed study and analysis of their contents.

A new product or service venture would generally be classified as a small business. Most small businesses are simply not suitable for professional investment funding. Consider these figures, which were compiled by the Small Business Administration (SBA) and the Internal Revenue Service (IRS):

Businesses filing tax returns (1983):

Proprietorships	10.7 million
Corporations	2.8 million
Partnerships	1.7 million
Total	15.2 million

Counting the number of small businesses in the country appears to be a tricky business. The definition of "small" varies by industry and depends on who does the counting. For example, Dave Hirschberg of the Economic and Research Division of the SBA states that "all but 1 or 2 percent of those businesses are small businesses, by any definition." This value, when applied against the total, showed a count of 14.9 million small businesses. However, the IRS came up with a count of 12.7 million.

No matter which figures are used, common sense dictates that an overwhelming percentage of the total number of businesses qualify as small businesses. The *Fortune* 500 lists the largest businesses in the country. In 1985 the smallest number of employees shown for any company on that list was 550. This figure is very close to 500, the maximum number of employees required for a business to be officially classified as a "small business."

Only a very small percentage of the 14.9 million small businesses use the professional investment community as a source of funding. We obtained the following figures for 1983 from Gerald Feigen of the SBA Office of Advocacy and a past administrator of the Small Business Investment Company (SBIC) program:

Venture-related funding placed	$2.8 billion
Average deal sizes	$2 million

From these data, we computed the number of deals made at 1,400 during 1983. Assuming that only one deal per company was made, only 0.01 percent of the 14.9 million small businesses was involved with venture funding.

Why is this so? One reason is that the overwhelming majority of business plans that reach professional investors are rejected, most without a detailed study and analysis of their contents. We observed two major reasons for this:

1. Investors tend to align themselves with business areas and people that they know. If you are outside that select group, your chances of finding a ready audience with a specific firm are slim.
2. Investors look for hot opportunities that have the potential for a return that will be as high as three to five times the original investment. Without the chance for a high return, your plan may get passed over.

As part of our research for this book, we sent a questionnaire to 2,500 company founders and professional investors. The questionnaires returned by the founders confirmed that most of them did not receive funding from any professional investment source. Rather they were funded privately, through family, friends, or close business contacts.

Other Ways of Funding Your Business

If only a small number of firms obtain funding from professional investors, one question comes immediately to mind: What happens to those firms, product ideas, or business plans that do not receive funds from professional investors?

To answer this question, let us look at some specific examples. Consider the CryoCold Company (the name is fictitious), a firm that makes cryogenic measurement instruments. (*Cryogenic* means super-cold, somewhere around the temperature of liquid hydrogen.) For several years, the firm, using cryogenic techniques, had been manufacturing precision instruments. Recognizing a market opportunity for measurement instruments in the manufacture of super-cooled semiconductors, the firm went to the venture capital community for financial help. Unfortunately, cryogenics left the investment community cold, and the firm received no financial support. So, CryoCold took other measures. By making deals with specific customers for future products that the company would produce, CryoCold proceeded to implement its opportunity.

In another example, a software firm sold a computer program package used to build advanced models of companies as a decision support tool. The firm believed that its product could be developed into an expert system for use by upper management or owners of medium-sized and small companies. The revised product was expected to have significantly expanded market potential, and the company went to the venture capital community for help. Unfortunately, it enlisted the financial aid shortly after a national conference of venture capital firms had been held, in which it was determined that software was "out." The software firm is currently proceeding along other avenues, funding its product development mainly through client consulting fees.

The point is that there are other avenues to follow beyond seeking financial help from professional investors. If your product idea or service is not well developed, is not in one of the currently hot areas for investment, or appears to be a marginal opportunity in its present form, you will need to look for these other avenues. You may be able to make deals that allow you to further develop your product, improve your market research, hire a management team, and prove the potential of your idea. Then, later on, when your product idea or service has been developed and proven, it may be easier and more fruitful to approach the professional investment community with a well-prepared business plan.

How Sound Business Plans Fall Through the Cracks

It would be nice to be able to say that a well-thought-out, financially sound business plan will automatically receive the evaluation it deserves. Unfortunately, this is not so. Even well-constructed business plans may fail to attract attention, as many of the stories we have heard can attest.

From our perspective, there appear to be three major reasons for this problem:

1. A lot of paper flows through the professional investment channels. Many business plans are processed each month. The people involved in the process of reviewing them are very busy and sometimes have difficulty answering even routine phone calls. Worthwhile projects can get lost in the shuffle.
2. A sense of status and power rubs off on the people who administer the investment funding process. These people each react in different ways. Most respond well, but occasionally an individual will misuse his or her position.
3. An in-depth understanding of an opportunity requires years of working experience and product knowledge. A number of the venture capital firms we encountered hire young MBAs to screen the business plans before a principal with the firm ever sees them. This can be frustrating for all concerned.

Most of the professional investors we encountered had taken great care to set up their operations so that everyone who approached them would be treated professionally. However, the problems we speak of do exist. Here are a few examples.

• An aggressive entrepreneur from Europe arrived recently in the United States. With a successful chain of stores back home, he felt ready to tackle the entrepreneurial environment in this country. Within a year, he had opened a retail jewelry store in an affluent neighborhood and was patronized by a steady clientele.

He and his partners developed a business plan revolving around a vertical expansion of their business. They reasoned that they would always cater to an exclusive clientele that would likely come to the prestigious location they currently occupied. With a focus on improving the business for these wealthy customers, the plan was sound and showed a well above-average return on investment with little risk.

In approaching a venture capital firm that expressed an interest in retailing, the man was rejected. "Your biggest problem," he was told, "is that you don't plan to go into suburban malls." He was left wondering whether the person offering the suggestion had read the plan at all.

• One of the authors and a business partner had a peculiar experience while dealing with a venture capital firm in the La Jolla area. We encountered a young MBA working for the firm as his first job out of school. He was excited. He had a good job and was getting married in a few weeks.

After presenting an idea that dealt with software and expert systems, the author and his partner disagreed about a particular point. Since both of us are skilled and have opinions, we argued the technical point.

The young MBA stopped the discussion. "You two will never get along. There's no point in continuing this discussion," he said, and ushered us out of the office.

• One group we observed was searching for a venture capital firm to review its business plan. They were told that a firm in Texas was looking actively for the type of product they were developing. Upon calling the firm, the group was told, "Before reviewing your plan, we'll require that you move to Texas." Can you imagine what else that firm would have required before funding the group's plan?

The Importance of the Business Plan Process

What is the moral of all this? Is the search for funding so confusing and frustrating that you might as well give up before you begin? Not at all!

On the contrary, you must enter the business planning process with the right attitude and have realistic expectations.

Dr. Marshall Burak is the Dean of the School of Business at San Jose State University, San Jose, California. He serves as consultant to several of the *Fortune* 500 firms. He has also aided and participated in startup companies that have been through the funding process. He has had a unique opportunity to observe the professional investment community at work. When we interviewed him in preparation for this book, he offered some advice to the would-be entrepreneur about the funding process. "When going after money," Burak says, "it is unrealistic to expect very much help from the venture capitalist in terms of management assistance. Even though they mean well, and they say they'll put someone on your board, the people are not generally available when they're needed. They try to impress the person they're funding with their skills, and they sell their support services. They're not on scene to help spot major problems as they evolve.

"You must assure your own success. Do everything and anything you must to see that your venture succeeds. Bring the best people you can find into the venture, and build a complete management team.

"Do a very comprehensive business plan for your venture, including all aspects of product development, manufacture, marketing, and distribution. Include every cost you can think of. Once the plan is complete, track actual performance against it as a basis for operational cost control."

You should realize that, since the professional financial community is so demanding and at times difficult to deal with, it is up to you to prepare thoroughly when approaching any firm in your search for funding. The complete and detailed description of the business planning process provided in this book will ensure that you are ready for any curve ball that may be thrown.

Next, be aware of the importance of flexibility. Each audience for your business plan will have different criteria and varying needs. In this book, you will learn to tailor your business plan and your presentation to meet the needs of each of the audiences you are approaching.

Keep in mind the many alternative ways of starting and developing your business. As already suggested, obtaining funding through the professional financial community is only one of several options. However, no matter which route you finally choose, developing a strong business plan as outlined in this book will help you enormously.

Finally, be aware that the post-mortem is a key step in the business planning process. When the response to your business plan arrives—and it may be negative—resolve to learn from it. Use what you learn to make your next business planning effort more successful. Above all, do not give up—especially if you feel very discouraged. As the farmer said when asked why he was digging in a big pile of manure, "There's got to be a pony in there somewhere!"

How This Book Is Organized

The business planning process starts with an analysis of the raw materials that go into the plan. It involves selecting the appropriate audience for the plan and tailoring the plan to suit that audience. It involves preparing and presenting the plan. Finally, in the event of rejection, it involves a "post-mortem" to determine what to do next.

No process can in and of itself guarantee success for a business plan. A bad product choice, a weak management team, or a poor financial opportunity can kill even the best-written plan. But you can improve your chances of success by finding the appropriate audience and identifying potential problems with your business plan.

Here is a look at how we shall be guiding you through the business plan process.

In Chapter 1, "The Business Plan: Why and How," we discuss several reasons for writing a business plan. The obvious reason, of course, is for funding. It is not so obvious that a business plan can simply help you run your firm or propel your product idea or service into existence. If you never present your plan to anyone outside of your firm or product team, you can benefit from preparing a business plan. You may want to prepare it for that reason alone.

The questions of market size and market potential are addressed in Chapter 2, "Define the Product and the Market." Many great product ideas have been created for what have turned out to be a disappointingly small number of customers. A product development team will almost invariably overestimate the potential market size and market share. It is unusual to find product developers who have thought through the process of marketing a product or who have conducted appropriate test marketing studies. The professional investment people you approach will demand some clear answers on these issues, and the founders of a firm or product developers should benefit from these answers as well.

The depth and quality of the management team can make or break any venture. In Chapter 3, "The Authors of the Plan," we discuss a self-assessment procedure that can be used by company founders or product developers. This procedure will assist you in determining what key management skills are needed and which ones are available. The motivations of the company founders and product developers are also important. Understanding what you want to get out of a situation can help in putting deals together. The answers to these questions are of interest to most of the people who will be receiving your business plan.

The selection of an audience for a business plan is one key to its success. We have identified a number of audiences for business plans beyond that of the traditional professional investor. In Chapter 4, "Choosing the Audience for Your Plan," we discuss several types of people that you can approach for help in trying to make your firm or product idea a success. By selecting the proper audience, you will receive the appropriate assistance to push your firm or product along.

When the initial data gathering is done, it is time to assess the basic ingredients needed for developing a business plan. In Chapter 5, "Assessing Fundamental Requirements," we offer a set of guidelines for determining whether a business plan should be written. This step is actually part of a process, and it is preceded by several steps relating to the gathering of information needed for a decision. Information on the market, available skills, the management team, and the potential audience for the plan is analyzed to determine if enough raw materials are available to justify writing the business plan. This bit of self-assessment can be used to spot missing elements in the plan to be written, and can save founders of firms quite a bit of time, energy, and potential disappointment.

The traditional components of a business plan are discussed in Chapter 6, "The Components of the Business Plan," along with modifications that might be useful for each of the audiences described in Chapter 4. The key is to tailor the business plan to suit the information needs and priorities of the audience chosen.

Often the business plan is the first encounter that any prospective investor has with the company founders, product idea, or service represented inside its covers. In Chapter 7, "Putting the Plan Together," we discuss the importance of the physical form of the plan and the first impression it makes. Completeness of contents, clarity of writing, accuracy, neatness, spelling, and grammar all count. They are your audience's first impression, and first impressions are hard to change.

In presenting a business plan, an individual or group is trying to attract the attention of some very busy people. Often the prospective investors have established barriers to exclude casual contacts, including you and your business plan. In Chapter 8, "Presenting the Plan," we discuss the presentation of the plan, from attracting the audience's attention initially to having the plan read with interest. In some cases it is easy, in others it is quite hard. Sometimes, it is best to be recommended by someone your intended audience knows and respects. This and other strategies will be discussed in this chapter.

In Chapter 9 we discuss a post-mortem. If your plan is rejected, you have two options: You can roll over and play dead, or you can keep looking for other strategies and other audiences. Our "after-the-rejection analysis" does two things: First, it helps you identify any true weakness in the plan which may have caused its rejection. Second, it helps you think through the next steps to take in pursuing your objectives. Once you have identified your next steps, you can use the process described in this book to gather more information, to select perhaps another audience, and to prepare a revised business plan. Eventually, you will succeed.

In Appendix A, we have provided a sample project plan. This plan serves as an example of the activities and time involved in a business planning effort. While your own business plan may take a different course, the sample provided will serve as a guide.

Appendix B contains another sample business plan, this one from Speech Plus, Inc., a real company that wrote a solid business plan and received funding. Although proprietary data have been disguised at the firm's request, you will find the plan interesting reading.

1

The Business Plan: Why and How

Having lost sight of our objectives, we redoubled our efforts.

Old Adage

In this chapter, we shall discuss why a business plan should be written and how, in general, the business planning process works.

The Process

In our questionnaire responses, many of the funders and several founders commented on the value of a plan. Nick Stanfield, President of MSI Capital Corporation in Dallas, Texas, spoke for many people when he wrote in a letter, "If there is one thing an entrepreneur manager needs to know it is how to write a business plan, and then have the discipline to follow it."

Many of the founders responding to our questionnaire said that they had written a plan, but it is now out of date and has not been updated in a while. Others said that no plan had ever been written. Not everyone sees the value of a business plan.

But a business plan, and the planning process that underlies it, can be a substantial aid to your business. It helps you to organize your thoughts and provide a clear set of long-term objectives. It helps you to focus your activities.

This is especially important when a number of individuals with diverse backgrounds are working together in a company or on a product development effort. It forces the creation and analysis of a strategy to reach the goals you set. It can help you to identify weaknesses in your product or service, your strategy, or your management team and allow you to define the steps needed to correct them.

The business plan is not a panacea. However, it does provide benefits in several ways. A full analysis of the market, the management, the finances, and the product is necessary to the health of any venture, and the planning process forces you to undertake that analysis. Without it, one or another of these areas may be neglected in the whirl of day-to-day operations.

The business plan organizes and focuses the energies of skilled people with diversified educations and work experiences working in a firm or on a product venture. Without a focus, the individuals concerned may not spend their time in the most useful and constructive ways to achieve overall goals.

The business plan, then, is a powerful tool for planning the long-term operations of a firm and for propelling a company out of its current situation and into another phase of its growth.

Who Should Write a Business Plan?

There are several types of businesses for which a business plan can prove beneficial.

An Individual with a Product or Service Idea

If you have a product or service idea of your own that you want to develop, plan on devoting much evening and weekend time and some of your money to the project. You can use a business plan, and the analysis leading to one, to review your product, its market potential, the type of management team that would be required if you started a company to produce the product, and the amount of money required. By sharing the resulting plan with a trusted friend or business advisor, you can gain an objective assessment of the project. If the idea is likely to be a real lemon, it would be best to know before you go too far with the effort. And, if it has a good chance of success, you may gain some supporters and some valuable assistance in the process.

An Entrepreneur Looking for Partners

A business plan will help you present your project and its potential to possible partners who may be able to help you in the venture. Each type of partner represents a potential *audience* for your plan.

There are different types of partners. A corporate partner may have the research, facilities, or even a computer system you may need to use. You could be looking for someone to market your product. You could be looking for possible members of a product development or management team. Each type of partner may have information needs that will vary from the standard business plan outline.

Business in Search of Capital

The business plan is mandatory when dealing with the professional investment community. To play "let's make a deal," the first thing investors look for is a complete, concise, and thorough business plan.

A Company Facing Rapid Change

If you manage an existing firm that is operating in an environment that is changing rapidly because of deregulation, your firm can benefit from the entrepreneurial opportunities that can be highlighted in a business planning exercise. Relaxation of government controls brings about a period of rapid change as well as a need and opportunity for innovation. In banking, energy-related businesses, the trucking industry, the airlines, and telecommunications, to name a few examples, countless opportunities have appeared since controls have been relaxed. The firm that can change its business to take advantage of the new business environment can survive the trauma and prosper, while those that do not will stagnate. In his book *Innovation and Entrepreneurship*, Peter Drucker voices the opinion that "Today's businesses, especially the large ones, simply will not survive in this period of rapid change and innovation unless they acquire entrepreneurial competence."

When firms have to change rapidly by identifying new products and services and moving to deliver them to their customers, the business plan is one of the best tools that can be used.

A Troubled Company

If your firm is having financial difficulties, or just is not showing the kind of performance that you want, a business planning exercise may help get you back on track. The process can help you develop new strategies or product lines, and also help you identify the areas in which your business may be organizationally weak.

Don't Make a Business Plan and Throw It in a Drawer

Many business people we have observed seem to do this. They view the plan as a one-time-only document, to be used for a specific purpose and then forgotten.

The firms that are most successful in following through on the process (and very often in conducting their businesses as well) view the plan as a living document. They update it annually, with more frequent updates if they're having problems. They continually work to ensure that the plan matches reality and that the goals and objectives it sets forth are achievable based on what they know.

The Process of Building a Business Plan

The process we are about to describe will guide you from the creation to the completion of a finished business plan for the audience, or audiences, you have selected. The steps in this process are outlined below.

Define the Product or Service

Start your business plan by producing a clear definition of your product or service, which a layperson can read and understand. Several funders we spoke with have indicated that a clear definition is very important to them. "Often," one said, "the people involved with a business plan write it for themselves. No one else can understand what they have and what they think it can do. It's a quick turnoff." Perhaps your product does something very arcane down deep in the bowels of a nuclear reactor that a layperson might not be expected to understand. If the layman cannot understand your explanation, though, you will never receive funding or assistance from any source other than a sophisticated investor knowledgeable in that specialized field.

By producing a clear description of your product or service, you may discover better ways to talk about it to prospective customers. In one instance, a firm found that the description it had prepared for the business plan was much simpler and clearer than the one it had been using in its marketing literature. They changed the materials and experienced a jump in sales activity.

Occasionally, a product definition exercise will lead to redefinition. Consider the example of a firm that sells window shades, which finds that its business is stagnating. The company might redefine its products as "light control devices." This strategic change opens up entirely new business areas that include venetian blinds and electronic dimmers, for example.

Defining your product or service begins by answering the following questions:

What does the product or service do?

Whom does it serve?

Physically, what is the product? (size, shape, color, packaging, computer hardware, machinery)

What is its value to the customers? Why do they buy it?

Can the customer use it immediately? Is training necessary?

Will the customer have to change the way he or she does things to use the product?

The resulting description should be understandable by *anyone*. As a test, take the finished description and give it to several people who have no prior understanding of what you are doing. (Be sure that they can be trusted to keep the material confidential.) If these people can develop a reasonable understanding of your product or service, then you have done a good job. (Chapter 2 contains additional material on product description.)

Define Your Goals

Define what you want to achieve from the business plan process:

Improved cash flow?

Improved profit?

Expanded market share?

A specific level of annual revenues?

Seed funding?

A public offering of shares in your firm?

Specified personal profit realized?

By defining your goals clearly and being as quantitative as possible, you set a benchmark against which the planning process can be measured. (The process of setting your goals and objectives will be discussed in Chapter 3.)

Analyze the Market

A key step in developing a product or service idea into a profit-making venture is to determine the size of the potential market and make some estimates as to the degree of market penetration you hope to achieve within a given period of time. It is easy to sit down with a pencil and paper, or a personal computer spread sheet, and run out a series of computations:

Potential customers		10 million
Selling price		$250
Market share:		
3 years	0.5%	50,000 units sold annually
5 years	1.5%	150,000 units sold annually
Revenue:		
3 years		$12,500,000 annual revenue
5 years		$37,500,000 annual revenue

A great deal of prior research should go into calculating these figures. By themselves, the numbers mean little to anyone who might consider investing in or working with your firm. You should do some additional research to answer at least these questions:

- Who, exactly, are the potential customers?
- How do you know they need or want your product or service?
- How did you set the price? (Did you use market price or another method?)
- How do you know whether potential customers will pay your price for the product?
- How did you determine your estimated market share?
- Is there anything that could prevent you from realizing the revenues and net profit you project? (Examples of such roadblocks are government regulations, unexpectedly good performance by competitors, unforeseen expenses, or loss of key people.)
- Where are potential customers located?
- How can you tell them about your product? (magazines, radio and TV, direct mail, etc.)

- What distribution channels are available? Can you get into those channels? If so, how?
- What type of customer service is required? How will you provide it?

These questions will appear again in Chapter 2. At this point, however, they can serve as a checklist for information needed about the market for your product.

Analyze the Management Team

You, your management team, and your technical staff must do whatever is necessary to achieve the goals you set. Therefore, it is important to review the skills that you possess collectively and the performance you have shown. For some people and firms, such an intensive self-analysis may be difficult. Sometimes only an outsider can have the objectivity that is required. Whether the analysis is done with insiders or outsiders, however, the insiders are the key to its final success or failure because they will be responsible for carrying the project through to a successful conclusion.

Although the questions to ask will be different in part for a startup than for an existing firm, at least these topics should always be considered in relation to your management team:

- Have you previously prepared a detailed business plan? Do you follow it? How often is it updated?
- Are sales volume, revenue, and expenses as high as you expected them to be? If there are variances, what is the cause?
- What financial shape is your firm in? Do you periodically run short of cash? Are taxes paid? Are loans current? Are payables current? How do basic ratios look?
- How happy are your customers? Do they recommend your product or service to others? Do they have complaints? How do you or your firm act on complaints? Do customers want changes in the product, or do they want a new product altogether?
- How happy are your employees? Is the employee turnover rate higher or lower than the average for your industry and area? What comments are obtained from employees during exit interviews?
- How often do employees contribute operational improvements or product suggestions? Are they enthusiastic contributors or, for example, do they think that the weekend is the best part of the week?
- How does your product or service measure up against the competi-

tion? What are you doing about any competitive weaknesses or opportunities?

- How effective is your marketing? What is your market share? What is the return on your marketing budget? What is the response to advertising? Do queries and sales leads come from sources you anticipated, or are unexpected responses being received? What is being done to capitalize on these opportunities? Is the marketing expense per unit sold and as a percentage of the total budget reasonable in comparison with other firms in the same industry?
- How are your operations doing? Have you done everything possible to minimize costs at all levels in the firm? Are improvements in your methods or technology possible? What would their costs and benefits be?

This list does not exhaust all the questions that could or should be asked to evaluate the management group, but it is a good start. There are more questions and additional discussion in Chapters 2 and 3.

Analyze What Is Needed Internally

Now that the product has been defined, the goals determined, the market analyzed, and the management team reviewed, you are in a position to decide what steps you can take internally to resolve any identified problems. (Chapter 3 discusses this process in more depth.)

Analyze What Is Needed Externally

Define the things that you are unable to do without outside help. This may involve financing, hiring, contracting for help, or entering into a relationship with another firm for technical, marketing, or operational assistance. Determine what sources are available for the kind of help you need, and define the audiences to which you will present a proposal seeking that help. (There will be additional discussion about this topic in Chapter 4.)

Analyze the "Raw Material"

Review the information you have collected in each of the areas discussed above. Develop a rating or a grade for each area, using the procedure outlined in Chapter 5. Determine whether the total combined grade is high enough to warrant approaching the particular audience(s) chosen and whether a business plan should be written at all.

Develop the Business Plan

Additional preparatory activities may be necessary before you start to write the plan. Marketing studies or customer surveys may be required as well as financial and operational analyses, and these should be completed before the planning process begins.

An exception might be when the audience for the plan exists within the firm. In that case the studies and tasks to be performed can be written as part of the plan.

When dealing with professional investors, it is best to lay as solid a foundation as possible on your own before approaching them. (A more in-depth discussion of this topic appears in Chapter 7.)

Present the Plan

The presentation of your plan to the selected audience is a critical step. If the plan is presented without thought and planning, your chances of even having it read in detail are reduced. Many of the professional investors who responded to our questionnaire deal primarily with plans that are referred to them by others whom they respect. Investors indicate that a very small number of unsolicited business plans are ever funded. Thus, if you first present your plan to, say, a public accounting firm, you may be referred by them to professional investors, thereby improving your chances of success. If you present it directly to those same investors first, however, your plan may not be read at all. (There is additional discussion of this topic in Chapter 8.)

Evaluate the Results

It is useful to analyze the result of a plan's presentation. Even if it was accepted, there may have been suggestions made that should be incorporated into the plan. If the response was negative, a "post-mortem" will be needed to identify the problems and the means needed to correct them before making the next attempt. (Chapter 9 describes this useful step in the process.)

Differences Between a Startup and an Existing Firm

The questions outlined on the preceding pages in the "Analyze the Management Team" section are primarily oriented toward an existing business. If a startup is involved, however, the emphasis of the questions should be changed. For example, instead of "How is . . . working out?" the question becomes "Who is going to do . . . and what is required?" Also, questions about the education, experience, and track record of individuals on the proposed management team become very pertinent in each area. The startup must identify which member of the team will fill each function described or implied, and that team member's training and experience will be relevant for a particular area.

CASE STUDY: Action Products, Inc.

Consider the following case study of a newly formed venture. The identities of the parties involved have been disguised at their request (and a fictional company name has been used) but the moral of their story should be quite clear.

The company, Action Products, Inc., sold a software/hardware product to the electronics manufacturing industry. The sales price was under $10,000 and the gross profit on each sale was well over 50%.

The management team was young and each one was a technical expert in the field. All but one member of the team had engineering degrees. The brilliant founder and president had developed the initial versions of the product, and was a true believer and a highly effective marketeer. The marketing vice president was skilled in the large company, large ticket sales arena. The chief financial officer, an accountant, was viewed as competent to keep the books, do the reporting, and maintain the cash flow. The manufacturing manager had had experience in large manufacturing firms with electronic assembly operations.

When Action Products discussed funding with venture capital firms, reference checks were made, the product was investigated, the management team was reviewed, market and sales results were studied, and investments were made. A substantial amount of funding was committed to the venture.

In a short time, Action Products was running short of cash, however. Sales were at one-fourth of projections, the company was losing several hundred thousand dollars a month, and customers were complaining about the quality and performance of the product. Creditors were angry; some of them were even interested in forcing the firm into bankruptcy.

Meanwhile, the principals of the firm had moved the operation into spacious new quarters, leased expensive company cars, and given themselves significant raises—even in the face of poor company performance. They were now spending their time on developing the founder's key ideas for curing the firm's ills while key problems in product development, marketing, quality control, and finance were not being addressed.

2

Define the Product and the Market

"Cheshire Puss," Alice began, "would you please tell me which way I ought to go from here?" "That depends on where you want to get to," said the Cat.

Lewis Carroll

To succeed with a product, you have to know your product and your market. To receive assistance from the professional investment community, clear and credible definitions of both the product and its market are required. These descriptions should be key items in the preparation step that precedes the writing of a business plan.

The material in this chapter is intended to be used *before* a business plan is written, to identify homework that must be done and to help in the decision as to whether a plan should be written at all.

The material in this chapter may appear to be of interest only to product developers in startups. But, if you are preparing a plan for use within an existing firm, the product definition step can be very important. This can be a worthwhile step in getting to a redefinition of product lines, new views of your products and customers, and new or revised product ideas.

In this chapter the processes of product definition and market definition are covered, two case studies are presented, and checklists are provided for use in collecting information to be used in both product and market descriptions.

Define Your Product or Service

If you are developing a product, and plan to write a business plan, then a clear, comprehensible product definition will be important to your plan's development. Consider this statement made by a principal in a large venture capital firm: "Whenever I get a business plan in which the founders weren't able to clearly describe their product, I think maybe they don't know. The plan goes in the wastebasket." Thus, an effective product definition is crucial to your business plan.

The product definition will do more than influence the various audiences for your business plan. It will become the basis for your marketing literature and will affect the rate at which your product penetrates its market. You should, therefore, spend as much time as necessary writing this description. It should be short, easy to read, and make the major points with a minimum of rhetoric. Unless you are sending the plan to someone who is a specialist in your area, assume that you are writing for the layperson. The jargon that you and your co-founders are accustomed to will have to be replaced with words that nonspecialists can understand. If this is impossible, then very careful, clear definitions of all technical terms must be provided. If the list of definitions gets too long, the description is probably too technical. In that case, you may want to consider enlisting the help of a professional writer.

Topics to Include in a Product Description

Many topic areas can be included in a product or service description, depending on your industry and the type of product. In the list below, we suggest a simple set of general categories of information that should be included.

What does the product do? What does the service deliver? A clear, nontechnical description is best. "Depositing a thin film of metal" is clearer than "sputtering." "Removing unwanted substances from water" improves upon "purification of water by filtration and deionization." Include a brief paragraph or two on the technical aspect if appropriate for your industry and product, but only *after* you have composed the version that will be understandable to your audience.

What is the product? Describe the product's physical characteristics clearly, including such features as size, weight, packaging, and color. State whether it is a machine tool, for example, and if it applies to computer hardware or software. If you are selling a service, define the nature of that service. Is your service delivered by consultants or in a training class? Or, is it presented in some other form?

Who are the customers? Describe the people to whom you will sell your product—that is, those who will make the actual buying decision. In cases where the buyer and the ultimate user of the product are different, the relationship should be spelled out. For example, a midwest firm sells a computer-driven audio terminal to telephone companies, which will replace information operators. Although the telephone company is the customer, the ultimate user of the equipment will be anyone calling the telephone information number.

What makes this product different? What distinguishes your product from other similar products? What will this difference allow your customers to do that other products will not? How does this product compare with the competition?

How complex is the product from the user's point of view? Write a *user view* of how the product is used. Keep in mind that a product can be internally complex as long as the user view is quite simple.

Can the product be tried with little risk? If the product can be tried at little or no cost, and without a significant investment in time, its chances of receiving a trial and ultimate acceptance are improved. Describe how this can be done.

What are the results of using the product? Does your product make something faster, better, easier, or cheaper? Your ability to describe and demonstrate these results is important in marketing your product.

Why will the customer buy the product? The reasons you state here may or may not differ from the benefits or results obtained from its use. If they are different, you should be aware of the difference (or differences) and identify and explain it (or them) in the product description.

What type of training is required to use the product? Describe the training required by a customer before your product can be used.

What regulations are relevant to the use of the product? This includes everything from product liability laws and environmental regulations to tax laws and zoning restrictions that may affect your product's definition and market. Explain how these regulations will affect both your firm and the customer. You may want to consult your attorney on this issue.

Stages of Development

The stages of development of your product idea or service will affect the kind of assistance you need and the audiences you can approach. Product development stages may vary among industries. You should attempt to define a specific sequence of development milestones for your industry, and then identify where your product falls in that sequence.

A list of stages for an engineering-oriented product might look like this:

Concept Formulation   This is the stage at which ideas and concepts for new products are first created. At this point, the product is non-existent.

Concept Testing   When a concept has been defined, it can be tested in numerous ways, including surveys, focus groups, discussions with experts in the field, and presentations to potential customers. These concept-testing procedures can help to give form to product ideas. If not done carefully, they may also give away the product idea. Use care to preserve your secrets, deal only with people you trust, and call in expert help when needed.

General Design   At this stage, the overall characteristics and capabilities of the product are defined. General requirements for development, fabrication, and testing are known, and general high-level drawings may be made.

Detailed Design   Specific detailed drawings are made up. Component parts and procedures for their assembly are specified.

Prototype   A working model or first sample is prepared.

Limited Production Run   A limited number of production models is produced, either by hand or by the creation of a small production facility.

Test Marketing   Marketing in a limited sample area is performed to determine customer reactions, to get feedback, and to identify any changes that might be needed.

Full Production   Final production runs to produce goods for sale are begun.

As your project reaches advanced stages of development, your chances of getting serious funding improve. Although some professional investors will provide seed money for the early stages, this is rare. Most professional investors prefer to enter the picture when the product development is complete. However, when a product is in the early stages cited on this list, it is possible to enter into creative deal-making with audiences other than professional investors, which can often speed up your progress.

Identifying where your product is on the above list can help you project your next steps and to choose the appropriate audiences for your business plan.

Testing the Readability of the Product Description

When you have completed your product description, including a discussion of the product's developmental stage and the next steps required, give the material to a trusted associate—preferably one with a minimal knowledge of your product. In addition, an accountant, a lawyer, or an investment advisor would be likely to read the material as a potential investor would, and his or her comments could be helpful. Also, all the large accounting firms have small business advisors who may be able to help you. In our experience, the firms of Deloitte, Haskins & Sells, Arthur Young, and Peat Marwick have been very helpful. Such firms are occasionally willing to devote a certain amount of time to your project, depending on the business climate when you approach them.

As mentioned earlier, take care to preserve your secrets when having a business plan reviewed. You must trust the other party or parties completely before you give them the material. Allow no copies to be made unless you are convinced that they will be treated confidentially, and use a nondisclosure confidentiality agreement if possible.

If after reading your description your outside reader understands the product, its benefits, and the work that needs to be done in the next stage, then you have done your job well. If these reviewers have questions, used them to guide you in reworking the material.

CASE STUDY: The EXUS Corporation, Product Description

Throughout this book, sections of the EXUS Corporation business plan have been included where appropriate.

The EXUS Corporation was formed to manufacture and market a leisure high-tech product combining exercises and the home computer. The EXUS business plan will be used in several chapters in this book. The

EXUS PLAN (1): PRODUCT DESCRIPTION

JOGGER

The first product that we will manufacture and market during the balance of 1983 is "Jogger."

It is video software on cartridge for the Atari 2600VCS.

"Jogger" was written to take the boredom out of running. There are two oval tracks on the television screen. The top track is the slow track and the bottom track is the fast track. In each track there is a red pace bean which travels around the track at a regulated speed. A pink bean is placed on the slow track, and is the object that is controlled by the "Foot Craz" activity platform (see below).

A person jogging on the blue and orange dots of the activity platform will cause the pink bean to travel around the track. The faster one jogs, the faster the pink bean travels. One must not pass the red pace bean until it has changed to a green color. By stepping on the red platform dot, the pink bean will be transferred to the fast track. If the yellow platform dot is stepped on, the pink bean moves back to the slow track. Number of laps in each track, total time and laps, and score are displayed on the television screen. This program becomes very challenging as the score reaches higher levels. Competition between "joggers" is inevitable.

FOOT CRAZ ACTIVITY PLATFORM

"Foot Craz" is the video foot controller, or activity platform, that activates play. It is the companion product for the "Jogger," and will be sold with software cartridge.

Using the feet, one can control various aspects of a video exercise program, while developing eye-to-feet coordination, agility, and the respiratory system.

Construction:

The "Foot Craz" platform is a 30″ x 24″ x 9/16″ two-ply foam pad. There are five flat, normally-open switches sandwiched between the foam plies. An Atari-like plug and cable are connected to the switches and routed out of the foam pad at the center edge of the 30″ side. To show the location of the imbedded switches, a nylon "pillow case" with five different colored 3 in. dots are in alignment with the switches.

Attributes:

The foam pad is light-weight, which represents savings in shipping. It can be rolled up to save on bulk rates. The construction is simple and does not require skilled labor. The materials are common and easy to obtain. The nylon "pillow case" can be pulled off the foam pad for washing.

plan is brief (51 pages), clearly written, and will serve as a reasonable example of a successful business plan.

Using this plan, EXUS received first-round funding. The product descriptions for two EXUS products—"Jogger" and its companion product, "Foot Craz Activity Platform"—are shown here.

Define the Market

A market analysis and definition can be useful both to the individual with a product idea and to the management of an existing firm. Both of these items will help you determine how much of your product or service you can sell, where you can sell it, and at what price it can be sold. It can also tell you what you need to do to get the product to market. This information is important in determining whether to proceed with preparation of a full business plan.

Within an existing firm, the market definition can be used for a new product introduction. It can also provide a fresh analysis of your existing market in that it identifies potential new customers and better ways to reach established customers. Of special interest are the customers you identify that are entirely unexpected, and the prospects that you have lost for no apparent reason. Investigation of these customers can lead to significant opportunities for growth.* Also of interest are significant weaknesses or strengths in the products or customer relations of your competitors.

Topics to Include in the Market Analysis Process

Here is a general list of areas that are of interest in a market study. Key topics may vary by industry and product. As you will see, the questions are oriented toward the need for proving to a skeptical observer that a market for your product exists and that the customer will pay your price. Various methods that can be used to accomplish this are mentioned in the list and described in detail later on in this chapter.

* See Peter F. Drucker's *Innovation and Entrepreneurship* (New York: Harper & Row, 1985), pp. 37–58, for a discussion of unexpected success or failure as one of seven sources of innovation.

Who are the customers? Identify this market in specific terms. Define such characteristics as age, sex, marital status, income, job position, and the effect of your product on their job functions. You are seeking as complete a definition as possible for the person or firm that will buy your product.

How do you know these customers want or need your product or service? Identify magazine articles and books, library research data, market gap analyses, focus group results, customer surveys, or any other data that can help prove that the demand for your product or service is real. If you have done some studies, gather and present the results; if not, identify the studies you plan to do.

How did you, or how will you, set the price? Consider your pricing strategy carefully. Is your proposed price based on cost plus a margin? Is it the market price? Is it based on replacement of functions? How do the competitors normally set their prices? Will your pricing method give you a competitive advantage?

How do you know the customers will pay your price? As with the "want-or-need" question above, you need convincing proof that the customers will pay your price. Customer or prospect surveys, focus groups, mail-order presale, and test marketing are several ways to develop this aspect of your business plan. Another good way, of course, is to present a significant number of orders from customers. It is hard to argue with signed purchase contracts.

How did you determine the market share you hope to achieve? As one venture capital professional told us, "It's the easiest thing imaginable for a firm seeking funding to say 'There's a big market out there, perhaps 10,000,000 people. All we want is 0.1% in the first year, or 10,000 units. That will carry us nicely.' That just doesn't cut it for we investors." Rather than talking about vague estimates, you need credible data to indicate how far you expect to be able to penetrate the market. Again, focus groups and surveys can be useful if the participants are carefully selected.

What might prevent you from reaching your sales goals? Consider such possibly troublesome factors as a sudden change in materials prices, changes in government regulations, new trends in liability law, and changing customer needs or wants. Which factors apply to your industry, and to what extent? What do you plan to do about the more significant ones?

Where are the customers located? How are the potential customers distributed geographically? Will they come to you, or will you go to them? What impact will their locations have on the sale of your product?

How can you tell the customers about your company and your product? Identify the most effective means of communicating to potential customers that your firm exists and your product is for sale. Are there roadblocks that will prevent communication with the customer? In the computer software industry, for example, marketing and distribution channels are so saturated with information and products that getting a new product through the maze is exceedingly expensive and the results uncertain. How can you overcome such barriers?

How can you get the product to the customer? Will you use the U.S. postal system, delivery by service personnel, a retail location, or some other means of distribution? What impact could this have on sales? What costs will be involved? Answers to these questions will determine attributes of your sales agreement with your customers.

What customer service is required? What continuing services are required to support your product? What services does the market expect? How can you provide them?

Who are your competitors now? Who will they probably be in five years? How do the competing products and services stack up against yours? What are their strengths and weaknesses? How can you capitalize on their weaknesses? What strategy or strategies will you use to deal with their strengths?

You may or may not be able to collect all the market information described here. However, the more you can present in your business plan, the more realistic and effective the plan will be.

Product Life Cycle

Product life cycle refers to how long will a product last once it is introduced. This is an important factor in marketing a product. The typical product life cycle in your industry can be a valuable indicator of what is likely to happen to your product. Most products follow a cycle represented by the graph in Figure 2.1, in which the introduction, growth, maturity, and decline of a product are illustrated.

Do some research to find out what has happened to other new products in your industry. Use the experiences of those companies as part of your analysis when preparing your market forecast. The key factors causing the decline of comparable products or services are of special interest and may have a bearing on the fate of your venture.*

* Additional discussion of product life cycles can be found in many marketing and management texts. One such source is Philip Kotler's *Marketing Management: Analysis, Planning, and Control.* (Englewood Cliffs, N.J.: Prentice-Hall, 1976), Chap. 11.

Figure 2.1 Product life cycle.

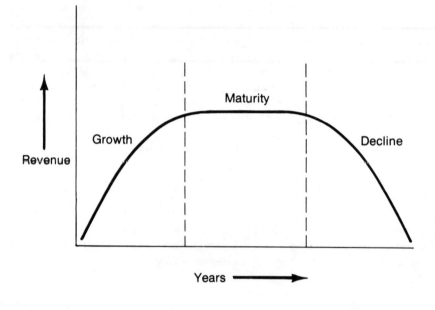

Methods of Data Collection

There are several methods you can use to gather the types of information needed in the "Market Description" part of business plan development. Some of the more popular ones are described below.

The Market Research Firm

If you have the money to hire one, a market research firm can conduct the various studies required to define the market for one or more products within an industry. You will have to spend enough time with the researchers to ensure that they understand what you are after, that you understand what they intend to do, and that you know what results you may expect.

To locate a market research firm, ask firms with well-designed marketing campaigns for referrals. If a recommended firm does not perform market studies in your field, ask them for a referral. Market research firms also advertise in trade journals and may have a display booth at trade shows. A good business school will have ties with some of these firms, and may even be able to recruit graduate students to do the basic work under the direction of an experienced professor.

The SCORE Program

The Small Business Administration sponsors the Service Corps of Retired Executives (SCORE). Through this organization you may be able to locate someone with marketing expertise who can guide you through the process of locating needed information. The possibility of obtaining help through SCORE depends entirely on the individuals who are available through a specific office. Do not discount this source of help until you have learned who is available in your area.

Library Sources

Your public library is a great source of market information. Trade journals for your industry can tell you about products, trends, and problems. Newspapers and magazines can be researched to identify topical information about the industry and your competition. Through financial publications such as those issued by Dow-Jones, Standard & Poor's, or Moody's, you may be able to learn about your competitors' organizations as well as their finances and their executives.

In the legal section of the public library you can review the environmental rules, product liability laws, governmental regulations, and other information pertinent to your firm and product. Of course, this form of research does not take the place of a relationship with an attorney.

In one instance the authors of this book did some preliminary legal research, which angered the attorney with whom we were dealing. His reaction was, "What am I—chopped liver?" We never worked with him again. We still contend, however, that it is best to be as knowledgeable as possible about legal issues when working with an attorney.

A well-stocked public library is also a source of valuable statistical information. Many publications, such as the annual *Statistical Abstract of the United States*, provide data on population trends, labor and business, income and spending, jobs and housing, geographical shifts, and so on. A skilled market analyst can derive useful forecasts as to how the market for a particular product or service is likely to change over the next few years.

In addition, do not overlook the *private* libraries in your area. Many corporations maintain business libraries, and you may be able to get permission to use one on a reference basis. Also, local universities and business schools maintain libraries, which may be worth checking as well.

The reference librarians are the best resource in the library, especially if your time is limited. Explain what kind of information you are seeking, and they will tell you whether it is available in the library and where to find it.

The Securities and Exchange Commission (SEC)

If your competitors have offered stock for sale or other forms of public securities, they were required to disclose everything about their firm to this government agency. Although trade secrets are excluded, nearly all other information is available. Product descriptions, marketing strategies, financial data, organization, executive biographies, all relevant contracts, and current or pending lawsuits are available for you to read. For one firm we researched, even the building leases were included. If it had mattered, we could have figured out how many square feet of space that company occupied! The local SEC office will allow you to read through microfilm records, and will explain several options you have for obtaining hard copies of any materials you are interested in.

Online Database Retrieval Services

Dow-Jones, Warner Computer Systems, and Standard & Poor's maintain extensive files which can be accessed through nationwide communications networks and used in the research process. Through Dow-Jones, for example, you can retrieve:

News headlines and full text from *The Wall Street Journal* and *The Washington Post* dating back to January, 1984

Items from *American Banker, Forbes, Financial World, Barron's,* and the *PR Newswire* dating back to January, 1985

Dow-Jones News: Broadtape and selected stories from *The Wall Street Journal* and *Barron's* dating back to June, 1979

Extracts of information filed with the SEC for over 9,400 companies (claimed in their User Guide), including corporate addresses, names, compensations of officers, and other hard-to-get information

Transcripts of the PBS television program *Wall Street Week*

Media General Financial Services detailed corporate and industry financial and performance information

The *Academic American Encyclopedia*

Using Warner Computer Systems, it is possible to obtain a full company profile report on most publicly held companies.

Using Standard & Poor's online systems it is possible to research individual companies or spot industry or consumer trends.

All of these services can be accessed individually. An interested researcher can simplify the process by using The Equalizer, a computer program available from Charles Schwab & Co., Inc. for the IBM PC or compatible hardware. This program coordinates all the phone numbers and does all the communications work necessary to obtain the services described above. In our experience, the program takes an unnecessarily long period of time to order and have installed, requiring much administrative back-and-forth with Schwab to complete the job. Once implemented, however, the time saved in research can be worth the wait.

Customer Interviews

Existing or potential customers are a good source of information about product and service needs and wants. They can tell you about the strengths and weaknesses of competitors as well as of your own firm. They can also listen to your product ideas and give you their reactions. This can be done in person or over the phone. (Telephone interviews will probably produce maximum information in a brief time.)

Suppliers

People who sell products to your competition or who sell related products to the customer set you are pursuing, can be an important source of information as to where the sales prospects are located and what they are buying. These sales representatives may also have some information on your competition.

Firms with Related Products

Firms whose products are not in direct competition, but may be indirectly related to the product you are researching, can provide additional customer and market intelligence. Use this approach with caution though, being careful not to reveal a good product idea.

Trade Associations

As you can affirm by taking a quick trip to the public or private library, there is a trade association for practically any industry you can think of. Trade associations inform people about upcoming conferences and create communication links among workers employed in the same field. At trade association meetings, people can exchange ideas, methods, and general information. These organizations even allow for social and recreational activities, although this is not their main purpose. Because trade organizations are an excellent source of intelligence about particular industries and the member activities, they should not be overlooked.

The Focus Group

It has become popular to arrange for groups of potential customers or industry experts to convene in order to discuss in depth a particular business or product. If properly conducted, such "focus groups" can produce credible information about problems to be solved, products that are needed, and likely customer reactions to a particular product.

A considerable science has developed around the use of focus groups, and you may want to consider using a firm of outside specialists to help. However, you can conduct your own focus group meetings on a more informal basis fairly easily. First, make sure that any experts you select are not also working for your competitors. Second, try to choose a representative cross-section of potential customers to participate. Finally, avoid leading or influencing the group discussion unduly. Otherwise, the session can be a costly way of bolstering a product decision that had actually been reached beforehand.

The Questionnaire

You can develop a questionnaire and buy, rent, or develop a mailing list of customers and prospects. Study carefully the mailing list you plan to use. Find out how the mailing list vendor obtained the names and addresses on the list, how often the list is updated, and how accurate the information has been in the past.

Create a one- or two-page typeset questionnaire, and write a convincing cover letter. To solicit meaningful responses, include some open-ended questions such as "What products do *you* think are needed?" or "What do you think is the most important problem in your professional area?" Answers to these types of questions may provide you with additional product ideas. Once the questionnaires are mailed, count on a three-to-six-week response period, and a return of between 0.5 and 1.0 percent.

Advertising Presale

Place ads in appropriate trade journals, describing the product you intend to market. If the product can be ordered by mail, you might place an order form in the ad copy. If checks arrive, make copies and return them, uncashed, with an explanation such as "We appreciate your interest in our product. At this point, we are a little ahead of ourselves. It's a little too early to take your money. . . ." Actual orders, along with copies of checks, make a pretty convincing case to potential investors that a market for your product exists.

If you have found a really hot opportunity, your competition will be reading your ads and trying to find out who you are and what your product is. To protect that information, you may want to use a "dummy" company name, an answering service that answers with the dummy name, and a post office box address. You will inevitably be broadcasting your product idea, so time is of the essence. Once you start, you have to carry through quickly.

Trade Show Presale

For some products, you may want to invest in a display and booth for a trade show. You can pass out literature and/or show a prototype of your product. If the demonstration is convincing enough, you could walk away with some orders. In any case, you will probably collect a large number of business cards from prospects. Use these orders and cards as further proof of interest in your product.

If members of the trade show audience are knowledgeable about your industry and have spending authority, you may find yourself talking with potential investors in your product. In one instance, a firm dealing with computer graphics for surgeons rented a display booth at a surgeons' convention and displayed a prototype of its product. Several surgeons were very impressed and later became sophisticated investors in the firm as well as customers for the product. Check with your attorney about this approach. If you appear to be deliberately soliciting investors without registering any securities, you may discover that you have a legal problem on your hands.

Test Marketing

You can try producing and selling your product on a limited basis. Depending on the market you are addressing, this can be an expensive path to follow. However, test marketing will provide answers to many of the questions listed on the preceding pages in the "Topics to Include in the Market Analysis Process" section. Books and marketing consultants can also give you extensive information on the most effective techniques to use in test marketing.

Objective of the Market Analysis Process

The goal of this effort, of course, is to produce a market description that is clear, complete, and credible, with as much backup information as possible. Given that information, it will be easy to prepare the kind of forecast computation shown in Figure 2.1 and convince anyone that a market for your product exists. You can expect the people to whom you present your business plan to check this information for themselves. Your information should make it that much easier for them.

Two case studies are provided below to illustrate the market analysis process. In the first case study, which concerns an ink manufacturer (Nor-Cote Chemical Company), the study process was informal and occurred over a length of time. In the second, which relates to a recreational equipment manufacturer (EXUS Corporation), the study was done as part of the business planning process. The second example is included word for word, exactly as the business plan was written.

CASE STUDY: Nor-Cote Chemical Company, Inc.

The Nor-Cote Chemical Company used several of the basic activities described above to uncover market information. (A detailed case study on Nor-Cote is provided in Chapter 4.)

The firm, based in Crawfordsville, Indiana, manufactures printing ink that is cured after printing by exposure to ultraviolet (UV) light. The main benefits to the customer are extremely rapid curing and reduced handling time. This in turn significantly reduces the time and cost of silk screen printing. The firm has been in business for nine years, employs 20 people, and has annual revenues that exceed $2 million.

Norman G. Woolcott, Jr., the firm's President, began studying the market for an ultraviolet curable ink in his spare time while working for another firm. "I wanted to see if I had a reasonable shot at it," he said during a recent interview. Market analysis has now spanned the firm's entire existence and is an ongoing activity. "In the beginning, it was very sketchy. At first, I had limited knowledge of who would use UV inks. I joined the Screen Print Association International, a trade association of screen printers. They had a list of members, and another list of the new members that joined each month. That gave me a good start. I talked with suppliers, and they told me in which regions they sold the most ink. I thought there must be more customers in those regions, so I began to develop some geographic information. I had informal discussions with consultants, industry experts, and personal contacts to gain more information. The manufacturer of the UV ink curing equipment we used was also willing to share data with us."

We asked Woolcott what he would do differently if he were starting over. "I'd pay a lot more attention to identifying customer needs and wants," he said. "Finding the customer is one thing, giving him something is another."

How would he find out about those needs and wants? "Just go and ask," he replied.

CASE STUDY: The EXUS Corporation, Market Description

Earlier in this chapter, we looked at the Product Description segment of the EXUS Corporation business plan. As you recall, EXUS was formed to manufacture a product that combined two popular fads: exercise and home computers. We shall now take a close look at another portion of the EXUS business plan: the market description.

As you read the following pages, you will note that many of the facts and projections have been invalidated by time. Both the home computer and video game markets have changed substantially in the few short years since the EXUS plan was written. This underscores the time-dependent nature of any business plan, and the need to review and update any plan you create.

Business opportunities are short-lived. Not only changing market conditions, but also economic trends, technological innovations, new competitors, and many other factors may affect the future prospects of a business idea. The typical effective business plan is written to fit a specific "window of opportunity," one which may remain open for only a matter of months. If an idea is to be revived a year or two after its creation, the business planning process must be reworked, with new conditions in mind.

Although the specific facts given in the EXUS business plan have been superseded by time, the elements that make the plan effective remain strong. That is, it is written in a clear, understandable style. It covers every point of importance. It is filled with specific information, usually in concrete numerical terms. And, the reasoning behind each of the authors' conclusions is presented.

The EXUS business plan was highly successful. Its authors obtained $3 million in funding for their business based on the plan. Today, the EXUS Corporation no longer exists. After its startup, a much larger company entered the field with a competing product and captured the lion's share of the market. However, the EXUS document remains a fine example of an effective business plan.

Checklist: Product Description

The following summary of topics to include in a Product Description can be used as a checklist for gathering required information.

What does the product do? What does the service deliver?
Who are the customers?
What makes this product different?
How complex is the product from the user's point of view?
Can the product be tried with little risk?
What are the results of using the product?
Why will the customer buy the product?
What is the product physically?
What type of training is required to use the product?
What regulations are relevant to the use of the product?

Checklist: Market Description

The following summary of information needed in a Market Description can be used as a checklist for gathering required information for a market analysis.

Who are the customers?
How do you know these customers want or need your product or service?
How did you, or how will you, set the price?
How do you know the customers will pay your price?
How did you determine the market share you hope to achieve?
What might prevent you from reaching your sales goals?
Where are the customers located?
How can you tell the customers about your company and your product?
How can you get the product to the customer?
What customer service is required?
Who are the competitors now? Who will they probably be in five years?

EXUS PLAN (2): MARKET DESCRIPTION

MARKET OVERVIEW

While the personal computer and video game markets have been regarded as separate and distinct by most market studies over the past several years, many new studies see the market as merging into a single continuum of computer products which are primarily differentiated by features and cost.

The game console has moved up in technology, while the personal computer product offerings have moved down in price to the point where they significantly overlap the game console pricing. Not surprisingly, entertainment usage is an important part of the motivation for purchasing low-end PCs.

At the same time, game consoles are being provided with keyboard options and memory expansion that will give them the ability to perform low-end PC functional tasks.

Personal computers will play games, and game consoles will do some personal computer tasks.

PERSONAL COMPUTERS

The figure below illustrates future personal computer sales performance over the five market segments to which PC products are applied.

Personal Computers ($200-$4,000)
Sales Distribution by Application

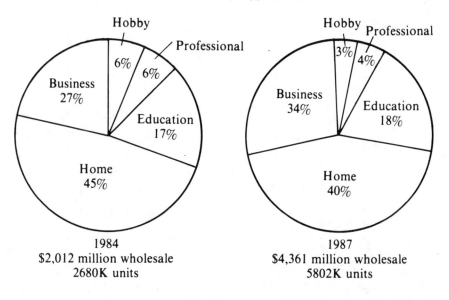

1984	1987
$2,012 million wholesale	$4,361 million wholesale
2680K units	5802K units

The suppliers of equipment to the 1982 and 1983 (estimated) PC market are as follows—$200 to $4,000 range:

	1982	*1983*
Apple	300KU	400KU
IBM	200KU	500KU
Tandy	200KU	300KU
Atari	300KU	300KU
Commodore	80KU	150KU
Osborne	50KU	100KU
Others	330KU	330KU
Total	1360KU	2080KU

HOME ELECTRONIC GAMES

The growth of revenue and unit sales from 1981 to 1985 is shown below. The forecast portion from 1983 on is based on the assumption that by 1985, 31% of the 85 million TV-equipped homes in the US will have an electronic game console.

The current penetration level is 15%. Some industry projections go to a 50% penetration level by 1985.

CONSOLE SALES

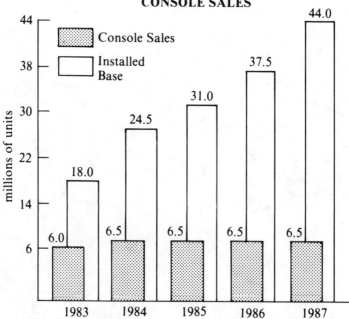

CARTRIDGE SALES

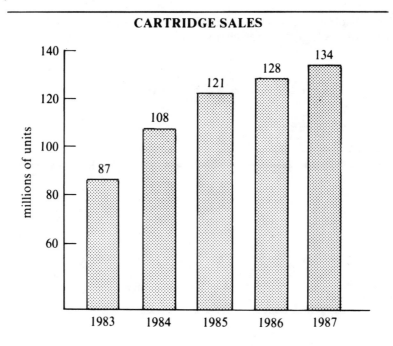

TOTAL WHOLESALE SALES DOLLARS

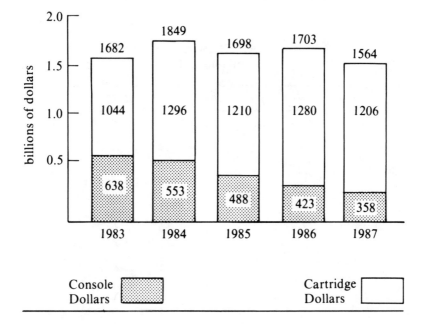

The console business has been dominated by Atari, and they will continue to maintain leadership for the next several years.

CONSOLE SUPPLIERS
(million units)

	Prior	1981	1982	1983	1984	1985	1986	1987
Atari	3.5	4.5	5.0	4.0	3.0	3.0	2.5	2.5
Coleco	—	—	0.5	1.5	1.5	2.0	2.5	2.5
Mattel	—	0.5	1.3	1.5	1.5	1.5	1.5	1.5
Magnavox and Others	—	0.2	0.5	0.5	0.5	—	—	—
Total	3.5	5.2	7.3	7.5	6.5	6.5	6.5	6.5
Cumulative Sales	3.5	8.7	16.0	23.5	30.0	36.5	43.0	49.5

In the game cartridge business, independent suppliers have focused on the Atari customer base. Activision reached $150 million dollars in sales on its third year in business.

GAME CARTRIDGE SUPPLIERS
(million units)

	1981	1982	1983	1984	1985	1986	1987
Atari	19	40	45	50	50	50	50
Activision	4	12	12	14	15	16	17
Imagic	2	4	7	8	10	11	12
Coleco	2	8	8	11	13	14	15
Parker Bros.	1	4	7	11	13	14	15
20th Century Fox	—	1	2	5	6	7	8
Mattel	1	3	3	4	6	7	8
CBS	—	2	3	5	8	9	9
Others	1	5	1	1	1	—	—

MARKETING STRATEGY

After a brief test in northern California, we will initiate a national drive to reach all business classifications that are potential customers for EXUS products.

Retail stores in 50 major markets will get our earliest attention. These markets represent almost half of all the households in the United States. It is quick. It is efficient marketing for EXUS, a new business eager for sales.

By the beginning of 1984, we will be cultivating the national chains, specialty stores, catalog and premium houses, direct mail syndicators, direct marketers, military sales, premium distributors, and incentive accounts.

We will also attend the major U.S. trade shows each year.

50 MAJOR U.S. MARKETS

Area	*Households (000)*	*Rank*
New York	3,514.7	1
Los Angeles-Long Beach	2,780.7	2
Chicago	2,538.6	3
Philadelphia	1,665.0	4
Detroit	1,534.4	5
Boston, Lowell, Brockton	1,323.8	6
San Francisco, Oakland	1,316.7	7
Washington	1,146.0	8
Dallas-Ft. Worth	1,138.3	9
Houston	1,110.1	10
St. Louis	854.2	11
Pittsburgh	838.7	12
Nassau-Suffolk	829.2	13
Minneapolis-St. Paul	795.8	14
Baltimore	780.9	15
Atlanta	766.0	16
Anaheim, Santa Ana, Garden Grove	736.6	17
San Diego	718.6	18
Cleveland	700.1	19
Tampa, St. Petersburg	683.1	20
Newark, NJ	681.6	21
Denver, Boulder	654.1	22
Seattle, Everett	644.4	23
Miami	640.3	24
Phoenix	598.3	25
Riverside, San Bernardino, Ontario	591.1	26
Milwaukee	513.0	27
Cincinnati	511.4	28

Area	Households (000)	Rank
Kansas City	508.4	29
Portland,OR	501.2	30
San Jose	486.9	31
Fort Lauderdale, Hollywood	453.5	32
Buffalo	448.6	33
New Orleans	438.9	34
Indianapolis	430.8	35
Columbus, OH	412.2	36
Sacramento	411.9	37
Hartford, N. Britain, Bristol	380.7	38
San Antonio	367.2	39
Rochester, NY	350.7	40
Louisville	334.0	41
Oklahoma City	327.2	42
Memphis	324.6	43
Providence,W'wick, Pawtucket	318.7	44
Nashville, Davidson	317.9	45
Salt Lake City, Ogden	316.8	46
Birmingham	315.1	47
Greensboro, Winston-Salem, High Point	311.9	48
Dayton	306.1	49
Albany, Schenectady, Troy	293.9	50
Total top 50 markets, households	38,962.9	

PRODUCT POSITIONING

Through 1987, A. C. Nielsen's Dataquest estimates that 581 million home entertainment video cassettes will be sold. During the same period, EXUS expects to capture one-half of 1% share of the market with sales of 2,693,500 units totalling $107,740,000 dollars

EXUS SALES PROJECTIONS
(Based on a wholesale of $40 a unit)
(Add 000s)

	1983	1984	1985	1986	1987	Total
Dollars	1,440	8,300	18,000	30,000	50,000	107,740
Units	36	207.5	450	750	1,250	2,693.5
Market units	88,000	109,000	122,000	128,000	134,000	581,000

Category

EXUS expects to achieve this goal by positioning its product line against the market to create a new category of video cassettes. EXUS products will be presented as *animated exercise systems that physically interact users with computers.* This statement will set EXUS apart from all others, as a business marketing a totally new group of products.

Name

According to Ries and Trout, who developed the first body of thought on "positioning," the single most important marketing decision you can make is what to name the business and its products.

We have chosen the Corporate name of "EXUS." It is a word much like "Atari." When first read, it made consumers wonder what it was. EXUS embodies a great deal of curiosity, as did Atari when it first appeared on the market.

EXUS is a contraction of "exercise United States," or "exercise us."

As a created name, EXUS should be securely protected as a registered trademark.

By using the theme line, "A new exercise system for us," the product reaches out and embraces the consumer. It says, "Hey, we all need to get in shape, and we, as EXUS are joining in with an almost patriotic zeal to help you become fit and stay healthy." Furthermore, it supports our positioning statement.

We could expand the appeal for the name with such promotional items as badges at trade shows that say, "Ask US about EXUS!"; bumper stickers that say, "I'm in love (heart symbol) with EXUS," etc.

Also, because of its Greco-Roman character, it implies strength, solidarity, and an athletic or Olympic root.

We are treating the tradestyle of the name in a modified script, much like the look of neon, to enliven our identity and appeal to activity-oriented people. The choice of product names like "Jogger", "Foot Craz", and "Stomp" contributes to this image.

Emphasis was given to the choice of the name at this point in our presentation to underscore the importance of it when conducting business in the consumer marketplace. One only needs to think of "Kodak" and "Coca Cola" to realize how important a name is in building a consumer brand franchise.

Packaging

The carrier of the "Jogger" cassette and the "Foot Craz" activity platform will enhance the distinctive character of the product and the further serve to position it. We will use a colorful, sturdy, and functional shelf carton that will have excellent instore visibility, strong display qualities, and prove to be a welcome convenience for the retailer.

Personal Computer and Game Console Sales Stimulation

The EXUS line is in an excellent position to stimulate the sales of personal computers and game consoles in retail establishments. As part of our marketing strategy, we will encourage retailers to display EXUS products next to PCs and game consoles to give consumers "reasons why" they should buy these supporting items. It is another reason why EXUS should find easy entry into the market and prove popular with store buyers.

Product Companionship

EXUS products have a special demonstration quality that can further contribute to retail store sales generation of other products. A wise merchandiser will display with EXUS products warm-up suits, jogging shoes, shorts, T-shirts, and other fitness-related goods. Other video cassette manufacturers do not have this EXUS advantage.

TARGET CUSTOMER

The table shown below charts distribution of sales by customer type, assigning a percentage to each.

Percentage of EXUS Sales by Customer Type

Customer Type	1983	1984	1985	1986	1987
National Retail Chains	5	40	40	40	40
Regional Retail Chains	5	12	12	12	12
Special Trade Classes					
Department Stores	40	17	18	19	20
Record Stores	2	1	1	1	1
Bookstore Chains	2	1	1	1	1
Drug Chains	15	5	5	5	5
Audio/Video Stores	3	1	1	1	1
Sporting Goods Stores	3	1	1	1	1
Discounters	5	5	5	5	5
Direct Mail Catalog	5	3	2	2	2
Direct Marketers	2	2	2	2	2
Direct Mail Syndicators	2	2	2	2	2
Anchor Premium Accounts	2	2	2	2	2
Military Sales	5	4	4	3	2
Premium Distributors	2	2	2	2	2
Incentive Accounts	2	2	2	2	2
	100	100	100	100	100

Through the balance of 1983, sales will be weighted to department stores and drug chains. This is due to our plan that will feed the bulk of the 36,000 sets produced to the West Coast markets. We want to insure prompt delivery, especially during the period November 15 through December 10. The Christmas season is hectic for stores. The closer and tighter our logistics can be during this time of our early development, the better chance we have of completing a profitable first-six months in business.

As the table shows, other customer categories will not be ignored in 1983.

Through 1987, the major customer type will be the large national retail chains, such as Sears, Penney and Wards. We expect them to account for 40% of our sales. This is good, reliable business from customers who pay their bills.

PRICING

EXUS products will have a wholesale price of $40 per set of one cassette (Jogger) and one activity platform (Foot Craz).

The recommended retail sales price is $79 per set. This gives the store nearly a 50% margin, which should be attractive since they typically look at only 40%.

As time and competition dictate, we will adjust our prices accordingly.

We will also entertain quantity discount proposals from customers, and if they are in the best interest of the Corporation, we expect to respond with a price adjustment. In such cases, each proposal will be scrutinized and evaluated on an individual basis. There will be no quantity discount policy, since experience has proven that the trade shows little respect for one, and tends to try for discounts on top of discounts. "I'll check with the home office" approach works best, for it gives us time to analyze each deal.

COMPETITION

In the literal sense, we do not have competition. We, as a product category, stand apart. However, we expect to see imitators by the middle to end of 1984. We shall deal with them effectively by having the flexibility to lower our price, while preserving our profit margins, and bring on line a steady stream of new, innovative products.

Indirectly, we have competition in all the video cartridge manufacturers because they, too, are vying for the consumer's dollar. Our prices are comparable to theirs, or better.

Competition is also represented by every other item for sale in a retail store, in a catalog, or sold through the mail. The consumer dollar has no conscience, no loyalty. It goes wherever the holder of it is duly motivated. Thus, it is the responsibility of EXUS management to its shareholders to cause sufficient consumer response for our products so that we reach our objective of one-half of 1% share of the market. We don't now see any reason why we cannot reach this goal.

DISTRIBUTION

As stated previously, we shall initiate sales in northern California during 1983. However, we expect to penetrate the national marketplace as quickly as possible by focusing on "targets of opportunity," many of whom will be concentrated in the top 50 markets, which represent approximately one-half of the U.S. households.

MERCHANDISING

EXUS will create the demand to "pull" our products through the retailer by a merchandising and cooperative advertising campaign, which will provide stores with a dollar allowance of up to 8% of their purchases upon proof of media advertising.

In addition, we will furnish retailers with highly-visible point-of-sale promotional display materials, reproduction-quality advertisement "slicks", logo sheets, radio scripts, TV storyboards, window banners, and in-store wire hangers.

To cap off our promotional support, we will provide detailed plans for product tie-ins, such as the 1984 Olympics; demonstrations; inner-store product "companionship" ideas such as "EXUS and dressed for jogging;" and seasonal events like "Indoor jogging with EXUS."

Our merchandising philosophy is firm. We want to relate directly our promotional expenditures to our sales.

We do not plan to spend money on regional or national media such as television, when our goal is to secure just one-half of 1% of the potential market. If our sales should exceed our projections, we can rethink our approach.

3

The Authors of the Plan

If, in order to succeed in an enterprise, I were obliged to choose between fifty deer commanded by a lion and fifty lions commanded by a deer, I should consider myself more certain of success with the first group than with the second.

Saint Vincent De Paul

Whether you are writing a business plan for use inside an existing firm or putting together a plan to obtain startup funding for a new venture, you will want to analyze the skills of your management team. This chapter is intended to provide an organized, objective process that you can use for this purpose.

There is a common set of functions that must be performed in every company. Which function you develop first is a matter of expediency. To have a well-run company, you will eventually have to cover them all.

The specific functions may vary by organization and their relative importance may change, but the same basic requirements remain. That is, someone:

1. Develops a product
2. Makes it
3. Sells it
4. Services it
5. Must manage the money
6. Must be the leader

The leadership role is perhaps the most important function of all. In our interviews and questionnaires, we saw that every successful and growing venture had one leader who believed in the firm and the product. The leader pushed, organized, cajoled, and otherwise *forced* the firm to exist and meet its objectives.

We also noted that a significant number of company founders had backgrounds and work experience in the technical or production ranks. When forming their management teams, however, people with marketing and financial skills were often not included. The founders commented on this in our questionnaires and interviews. For this reason, we emphasize the need for marketing and financial information in this book.

Toward the end of this chapter, the basic functions and skills of marketing and financial experts on management teams are briefly described. An analysis method is presented for reviewing the skills available to you in these areas. To illustrate a method of testing the management of a startup, the concept of interactive testing is also discussed. The organization chart from the sample business plan is presented. Finally, several case studies are included to illustrate the issues discussed.

Basic Skills Needed

There are many reference sources on the basic management responsibilities. Perhaps the best known of these is Peter F. Drucker's *Management: Tasks, Responsibilities, Practices* (New York: Harper & Row, 1973). While the basic tasks of management have not changed significantly in some time, the tools used by management and the speed at which management tasks must be performed have increased to keep pace with a quickening business environment.

Though the need for the basic management skills is recognized, it is easy to find organizations that do not have or use all of these skills. Often people with the "right" skills are ignored because of internal politics, the culture of the firm, or the limitations of the organization itself. Even in large and apparently successful firms, not all basic management skills are available and those which are available may not be used.

Consider this comment made by the president of an electronics manufacturing company, who was interviewed in the writing of this book.

> Our firm was working hard for a bulk sale agreement with
> a worldwide communications company. Our product was di-
> rectly addressing what for them was a critical need. It replaced
> labor in a business environment where the market shares were
> essentially fixed, the technology in use was old, and the com-
> petition was beginning to automate. Not to follow suit was
> suicide. The president of this potential customer told me, "We
> are a $5 billion per year company. Our profit margin is more
> than most companies hope for. Why should we do anything?"
> After almost a year of marketing, I felt like throwing him out
> the window.

Obviously, some critical, basic management skills were not being
applied at this major international organization. Unfortunately, that
company is now seeing its market share erode in favor of younger firms
that are adopting newer technologies.

In a startup, it is quite easy to ignore management responsibilities.
Management tasks do not get media attention whereas new technology
and innovative products do receive publicity. The new and exciting ob-
scure that which is merely necessary. While your efforts are being focused
on your product, the organization of your new venture—as well as strategic, marketing, and financial issues—may be neglected.

A Review of Skills Is Difficult
—But Crucial

In any company, a self-analysis of the basic management skills can
be difficult. Even if considerable care is taken, there are bound to be some
bruised egos and hurt feelings. However, if you wait until a professional
investor performs a due diligence study, this self-analysis can become a
real problem. ("Due diligence" is the name professional investors give to
their investigation of you and your business plan, and it will be discussed
further in Chapters 4 and 8.)

Consider the example of a small Midwest computer services company
(its identity is disguised) whose management staff believed it had all the
skills it would ever need to serve its longstanding customer base.

CASE STUDY: Fast Computer Services Company

Fast Computer Services Company was a wholly owned subsidiary of its parent corporation. It provided back office support for financial organizations. With 100 employees, $6 billion in annual revenues, and low operating costs, Fast's management believed that the firm was in a position to make some adjustments and improve its profit margin to approximately 30 percent. However, in order to make the needed changes, management would have had to buy Fast Computer Services away from the parent company.

The leveraged buyout process was studied and a consultant was brought in to assist. An experienced hand at analyzing organizations, this consultant had previously assisted several well-known firms in similar buyout deals. At an all-weekend meeting, the firm's management team became tired of the business planning process and began to insult the consultant. Why? The group was clearly stung by the consultant's implied judgment that Fast did not have the management strength to pull off a buyout.

"You're going to need a chief financial officer and an experienced marketing executive," the consultant said. "From the financial information you've given me, it's impossible to see the true condition of the firm."

The financial executive replied, "Those reports have been carefully developed with the parent company. That's what they want to see. They have been satisfactory for some time."

Fast's marketing executive was an experienced salesman whose only skills were in making sales calls and closing deals. When the consultant began to talk about such things as services delivered, target customers, market studies, and methods of expanding the geographical coverage of the firm, however, the marketing executive became very quiet and listened carefully. He said little for the remainder of the discussion and later indicated that the meeting with the consultant had been of little use and that the money spent on it had been wasted. At the end of the session, the consultant left and did not return.

Fast is still owned by its parent company and the operation continues as usual. The consultant reported to his associates and their network of contacts that it would be unwise to give financial support to Fast. The opportunity was lost.

In this example, it could have helped to have an objective review of Fast's management skills as part of a business planning exercise. However, the firm's management team would have had to be strong enough to accept the results of such an evaluation. In a startup environment, this kind of analysis can identify the balance of skills needed on the founding management team.

A Management Review Process

The review process can be broken down into four simple steps:

1. Start with a *general list of the management skills* and responsibilities needed.
2. *Customize that list* for your firm, reflecting on the specific needs of your product and market.
3. *Inventory the skills,* experience, and education of your management group or, in a startup, founders.
4. *Using a matrix format, map the skills,* experience, and education you currently have available in conjunction with the tasks and responsibilities identified as needed. Weaknesses or missing skills should be easy to identify. (An example is provided in Figure 3.1.)

Each of these steps is described below.

General List of Management Skills

A general list of management skills needed to cover basic functions is presented below. Although position or job titles are not critical, it is important that all the functions described are performed by your management group.

President or Chief Executive Officer   Overall executive skills are needed. Someone with a working knowledge of each area of the firm's marketplace and operations is needed. Strong leadership qualities and good communications skills and the ability to organize, direct, and motivate people are also needed. Another key skill is this person's ability to resolve conflict and keep the organization moving toward its goals. The person who combines most of these skills is often the driving force that makes the organization work. Organizations can function without these skills, but their successes will be slower and less assured.

Product Champion   Each product needs a product champion—that is, someone who is committed to the product or service and who is a zealot, a true believer in it. This person provides an independent force to propel product development and marketing. Often, products, services, and even internal projects lose their momentum and die without such a force behind them. The product champion is not necessarily the same

Figure 3.1 Sample mapping of skills to match needs.

Dreamware Video, Inc.

Skills Needed

Person and Function	Overall Executive	Leadership	Conflict Resolution	Writing	Speaking	Communication	Product Champion	Product Developer	Treasury	Controller	Marketing/Overall	Marketing/Sales	R & D	Manufacturing	Customer Service
Walter Mitty President	2	2	1	5	4	3	1	1	1	2	1	0	0	2	0
Gowan Getum VP, Marketing	4	3	4	5	5	3					5				2
I. Pinchem VP, Finance			3			1			0	5					
Ruby Goldberg VP, R & D				2	4	2		5					5	1	
I. Makem VP, Manufacturing	3	5	2	3										4	
Ann E. Oakleigh Customer Support	1	4	5	3	4	4									5

person as the overall leader described above, although the two roles may be combined. If they are, the president/CEO may make decisions from a product perspective rather than from a whole firm perspective. The function of "product champion" has no official job title and is not found on any organization chart, yet it must exist somewhere in the firm.

Financial/Treasurer Someone with these necessary skills must be constantly reviewing the future cash needs of the firm and tackling required fund-raising activities well in advance of critical situations. Many firms we have worked with describe this as a nearly full-time occupation. If your firm has received venture capital support, this function may be performed with help from the venture capital firm.

Financial/Controller The person with these needed skills prepares the budget, handles the payroll, processes accounts payable and receivable, maintains the general ledger, and provides financial reporting. He or she also establishes internal controls for expenses, administers contracts, and performs purchasing functions.

Marketing Specialist   Someone with marketing expertise is needed to identify markets and customers, to spot trends leading to new opportunities, to develop marketing strategy, and to develop and implement required advertising plans. The marketing specialist should be able to provide well-informed advice as to the kinds of products, distribution, packaging, service, and pricing needed to compete effectively in the marketplace.

Sales Manager/Staff   The head of this function should have executive selling skills, be able to build and train the type of sales force required, be knowledgeable in sales compensation, and be able to successfully motivate and manage the egos of his or her sales staff. Also helpful is a strong working knowledge of territory management, and of lead control and tracking, to insure that all leads are followed up and that sales personnel are actually fulfilling their responsibilities.

Research and Development Manager/Staff   Once a product is introduced, it will go through what seems to be an inevitable cycle of growth, maturity, and decline. Unless the firm plans for this, it will decline along with the product. The person or persons employed in this area must be able to work with the marketing, sales, and customer service departments; spot emerging product opportunities from both internal and external information; and produce the basic design for a new product or products. He or she must then work with product manufacturing to get the product into production.

Product Manufacture or Service Delivery Manager   In a product-selling company, the product is either made or purchased for resale. In a service firm the service must be delivered. A manager is needed who has a detailed knowledge of how this function is to be carried out. This person will carry the main burden of problem-solving in the product manufacture and may eventually supervise a large number of people.

Customer Service and Maintenance Manager   Once the product is sold, customers' questions have to be answered and service has to be provided. This function can make or break a firm in competitive environments where products are often similar in price and features. During our interviews, we heard more than once of the importance of customer liaisons and of "building a lifetime relationship with a customer."

Overall Planning, Budgeting, and Control Skills   All of the key people chosen to provide each of the above functions must have appropriate levels of experience in planning and budgeting, as well as in operational and financial controls.

Customize the List

Since every firm and industry is different, there is no set formula for changing the general list of skills presented above into the specific list required by your firm or business venture.

We suggest that you review each of the above skills and ask questions such as those listed below. Your answers to these questions will help you tailor the skills itemized in the "General List of Management Skills" section to your particular needs.

Does this skill apply to your firm? A company manufacturing a straightforward, low-tech product for the consumer market, such as garden hoses, may not need a research and development function.

Do we need the skill now, or do we need it at some time in the future? If needed in the future, consider what event or milestone will be your key indicator.

How can we reword the definition to fit our specific situation? Changes in wording may be needed to fit the jargon of your product and industry.

What unique skills are needed? If you are selling medical electronics, for example, it will help to have a medical doctor affiliated with your firm, to help define and provide the skills that are unique to your product and industry.

Inventory Existing Skills

List all the individuals on the management team of your firm or your startup's management team. Next to each name, list the individual's experience and education, together with an honest analysis of the results he or she has attained while performing the functions you need. In the case of a startup, list the results expected to be attained by each individual.

This can be a bruising process. To make it easier for the team members, you may want to have each person on the team describe and evaluate the others. The evaluation sheets can be typed, to avoid recognition of handwriting, and edited by an uninvolved person to ensure that characteristic words or phrases do not appear. The results can then be combined into a final list, representing the group's consensus evaluation of their own skills.

Using a Matrix to Compare Available Skills to Needs

Using a format similar to that shown in Figure 3.1, map the results from the steps above, in the "Inventory Existing Skills" section, into a combined matrix of "Skills Available/Skills Needed." The presence or absence of skills and an evaluation of performance should be included in the matrix.

In Figure 3.1, six officers in a nonexistent company have been analyzed. The skills needed to operate the firm efficiently are listed across the top of the matrix. The members of the management team are listed in the left-hand column. Scores for each individual in every area deemed important to the organization and to his or her current functioning are entered in the appropriate cells in the matrix. The scores range from 0 (indicating no experience and skill) to 5 (indicating a high degree of experience and skill). A zero means that the skill was deemed important for the function and person, but is not present. A blank cell means that the skill was deemed unimportant for the function and person.

Evaluate the Results

It is fairly easy to analyze the matrix. A column with no entry usually represents the existence of an important problem, unless the function has been identified as not needed or not needed now. A column with poor performance evaluations (0, 1, 2, or 3) for one or more functions also indicates the existence of a problem.

In the example, we see a company president who is expected to have at least a passing knowledge and experience in most areas of the company's operation, as well as reasonable leadership and communications skills. However, the person now serving is weak in many areas. Treasury skills are essentially absent, and marketing and research and development (R&D) skills are confined to one individual, which is an acceptable but risky situation.

You can develop your own scoring scheme, which may represent a variation on the plan shown here. However, if you do create your own matrix, avoid "subjective weighting" factors. These usually take the form of factors, often ratings ranging from 0 to 1 that are intended to indicate "how important this factor is to us." These factors are usually determined by a committee. Subjective weighting is one method that mediocrity uses to perpetuate itself. Your chances of success are improved if the strongest people possible are on your management team. Objective, candid self-analysis is essential to ensure that this is the case.

Act on the Needs Identified

Once your self-analysis is complete, take the action necessary to correct any serious weaknesses. People with the needed skills can be hired, training activities can be started for those already on board, and the need for one or more people with specialized skills can simply be identified and recognized in the business plan.

The Significance of Education

Many founders who responded to our questionnaires and interviews proudly described their accomplishments. Because of our selection criteria, virtually all were managing successful multi-million dollar companies, and some of their founders did not have college educations. In one case, the president had finished only one year of high school. Therefore, education is not necessarily a prerequisite for success.

All founders in our sample who received funding from professional investors had earned at least a bachelor's degree. Most had an advanced degree, such as an MBA, a Ph.D., or a J.D. It may be possible to obtain funding without a college education, but there were no such instances in our sampling. Education may not be a prerequisite for success, but it could be a prerequisite for funding.

Interactive Testing

This is an interesting method of testing a new management team for a startup or of assessing an existing management team. Suggested by Richard M. White in his book, *The Entrepreneur's Manual* (pp. 87 to 97), this approach requires you to gather your existing firm's or startup management team together in a motel over a weekend. Significant working assignments are distributed to the prospective or existing team members and are to be completed on short time schedules. These assignments call for both individual work performance and interaction with others. Pressured deadlines for completing the projects may cause tempers to grow short. In the process, however, natural leaders often emerge, communications skills become evident, and technical ability is quickly recognized.

The steps required for existing firms and for startup firms may differ slightly. White suggests the following steps for a *startup* operation:

1. Meet for Saturday breakfast. Describe your startup, your product, and your market.
2. Break the ice. If all the candidates do not know each other, have them introduce themselves to the group—describing their background and interest in the venture. Have them sign nondisclosure agreements as needed, and distribute the information that will be used in the testing process.
3. Have each candidate interview each of the other candidates. Observe the process to determine how the candidates interact.
4. Test departmental teams. Organize the candidates into the departments in which they are applying for positions. In one hour's time, each group should define its goals and objectives, set milestones and priorities, and determine a budget. Have each group send one member to the podium to explain the results of their meeting. Watch each group. Observe who is chosen to represent each group, and how the members interact among themselves. Note the skills and abilities that are demonstrated.
5. Test the organization as a whole. Step 4 may have forged some strong departmental teams while washing out some of the weaker performers. Now allocate about five hours to a set of assignments that require all the departments to work together in developing overall plans and budgets as well as reporting, controls, and administrative procedures. This step can be highly emotional, bringing out the best—and the worst—in the participants.
6. Have each participant fill out a ballot indicating his or her interest in working with the venture and identifying any individuals that he or she would *not* want to work with. Each participant should also place titles and job functions next to the names of the other candidates.

The collected ballots are used to determine strengths and weaknesses in the candidates participating, and to identify the strongest candidates for each position.

A word of caution is needed. Interactive testing can be an emotional, even painful, experience. Therefore, this step-by-step approach takes careful planning and preparation. You will want to read White's book before attempting this exercise. We didn't provide a separate list of steps for an existing firm. You can develop those variations on your own.

CASE STUDY: The EXUS Corporation Organization Chart

The organization chart segment of the EXUS Corporation business plan is included here. The names have been abbreviated and specific details that could identify individuals have been disguised. A case study for the DAVOX Corporation has been included, as well as case studies for Great Grains and CompuProcess (both names are disguised). The views of several business people who felt no need for a business plan are also discussed.

CASE STUDY: The Davox Corporation

This case study provides some good examples of financial deals with professional investors, of making a deal with your customers, and of the revival of a firm by reworking its management team. (This case will be referred to again in Chapter 4.)

Davox Corporation manufactures computer terminals that combine sophisticated communications protocols and display capabilities with voice access to standard telephone lines. The firm's customers are banks, credit card companies, and telephone companies, which benefit by increased productivity for knowledge workers. The company has annual revenues of $14 million and employs 100 people. Headquarters are located in Billerica, Massachusetts.

The firm was started on a research and development (R&D) partnership arranged by the venture capital firm of Hambrecht & Quist. Approximately $200,000 was raised at that time. After one year, additional funds were needed to get the product to market. A private placement was arranged by Hambrecht & Quist, and the R&D partnership was terminated. Three other venture firms were brought in as investors, and approximately $2 million was raised.

Davox began to run out of money at the end of its second year of existence. The investors were concerned, because no believable business plan was in evidence. The firm was operating with a research orientation rather than a business orientation, and significant additional funds would be required to bring its product to market. The funders concluded that the original founding team was lacking in the right mix of business experience and discipline.

Daniel Hosage is currently President, Chief Executive Officer, and Chairman of the Board of Davox. He was brought into the firm as a professional manager during the firm's third year of operation. He immediately began changing the orientation of the firm and solving their financial problems.

Another private placement was arranged contingent on changes to

(text continues on p. 69)

EXUS PLAN (3): ORGANIZATION CHART

MANAGEMENT

G.P. is the President/CEO and acting CFO of EXUS. He is the founder of ARGO, Ltd. a $9 million consumer products advertising agency. G.P. financed, managed, and promoted a popular trend gift item; was President of ABC, Inc., national marketing consultants; is associate professor, Journalism & Mass Communications, WEST University; and is the former marketing director of "SELL IT," Inc. He holds a Bachelor of Arts degree from WEST University. He will be working full time at EXUS.

P.J. is Vice-President of Engineering. He was a microwave engineer for APPLIANCE, Inc., and holds a Bachelor of Science degree in engineering from Eastern Technical. He has expertise in digital, analog, and microwave component and system level development. He is currently working full time for EXUS.

Q.K. is Vice-President of Marketing. He is currently with Department Stores as Director of Retail Merchandising. He will join EXUS when it is funded. His past experience includes Sales Development Manager for REPS, Inc.; Corporate Employment Manager for "SELL IT," where he was responsible for training sales staffs. He holds a Bachelor of Arts degree from WEST University and is a Lt. Colonel in the USMCR.

A Chief Financial Officer has been identified and is expected to join EXUS within 30 days of manufacturing.

M.S. is Secretary of the Corporation. He is an attorney and general partner of the law firm Fells & Meyers.

BOARD OF DIRECTORS

P.M.	Chairman of the Board
G.P.	President/CEO, acting CFO
S.L.	Director; Corporate Counsel
J.B.	Director; Vice-President, XYZ Corp.; Private Investor
M.B.	Director; Dean, West University, School of Business
I.K.	Director; President, Electric Corporation

ORGANIZATION

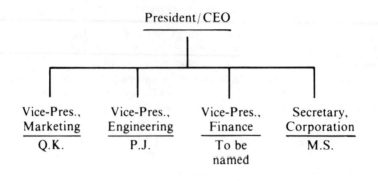

THE TEAM

The executive officers and directors of EXUS are as listed below. The common stock ownership shown is agreed upon and is planned to be in effect prior to funding.

MANAGEMENT

Name	Age	Position	Common Stock Owned
G.P.	54	President/ CEO	125,000
P.J.	29	Vice-President, Engineering	125,000
Q.K.	38	Vice-President, Marketing	20,000
M.S.	36	Secretary	3,750

REMUNERATION OF MANAGEMENT

Name	Position	Direct Remuneration
G.P.	President/CEO Acting CFO	$80,000
P.J.	Vice-President, Engineering	$55,000
Q.K.	Vice-President, Marketing	$55,000
To Be Named	Vice-President, CFO/Comptroller	$45,000

SUPPORTING STAFF

Name	Position	Direct Remuneration
H.S.	Manager, Engineering	$45,000
R.O	Manager, Plant Operations	$40,000
L.M.	Manager, Product Promotion	$30,000
G.B.	Executive Secretary	$20,000

PRINCIPAL SHAREHOLDERS

The distribution shown below is the intended distribution of the Corporation's equity by the founders. The Chief Financial Officer's position has not been filled at the time of the preparation of this business plan and, therefore, is shown as a statement of intent rather than fact.

Name	Type of Ownership	Number of Shares
G.P.*	Capital stock	125,000
P.J.*	Capital stock	75,000
Q.K.*	Capital stock	100,000
CFO*	Capital stock	25,000
S.L.	Capital stock	125,000
M.B.	Capital stock	50,000
J.B.	Capital stock	42,500
I.K.	Capital stock	50,000
P.M.	Capital stock	50,000
H.S.	Capital stock	3,750
A.M.**	Capital stock	21,250
M.S.	Capital stock	20,000
H.S.	Capital stock	20,000
	Total	707,500

*Founders
**Investment Company of

the existing management. Hosage was appointed as CEO of the company. The original Chairman had just recently hired a President and, with Hosage's appointment, both of them were moved aside.

In an in-depth interview, Hosage described the situation.

> It was difficult. Within the first week, it was obvious that there could be only one CEO. The President resigned, and we handled it as gracefully as we could. He got a year's severance pay, giving him enough time to find another job. Within three weeks the Chairman began to react. He finally realized he had lost his company. He became frustrated and resigned, taking a key technical person with him. At the end of three weeks, I had an interesting challenge on my hands: To complete the funding and replace key people.

Under Hosage's leadership, Davox successfully completed two deals that resulted in financing by their customers. Hosage describes each of these efforts.

> We sold shares to a major stock brokerage firm. They had a sophisticated, even enlightened MIS department, and were perfectly in tune with our product. We completed the sale of our product to the company, and they were impressed with our ability to modify the equipment to meet market needs. We had a confluence of the right factors. They saw we were trying to raise money, and they wanted "in."

> We then sold shares to a regional Bell operating company, a $4 billion operation. First, we went through the process of selling them an OEM agreement. They were going to sell our products in their marketplace. In the process, I met every major executive in the company. They had a small subsidiary which operated like a venture capital firm. They sat in on a few of our meetings. As we were about to consummate the OEM deal, they said they wanted "in." We raised $1.5 million in that transaction.

Today, the company has completed five financing deals and has five classes of stock. It has also successfully raised money every year.

The interview continued with a discussion about the management team, its skills, and its responsibilities. Hosage stated:

With any company like mine which is growing, it takes a tremendous amount of time on the part of the CEO to raise money. It's a time consuming, never ending job. You finish one deal and think you've got it done. But you look at your cash flow, look at where you're going, and you say "Oh my God, I'm going to have to do it again for next year." You get 90 days to breathe, 90 days to worry, and you start in again.

Last year [1985] was one of the toughest years I can remember. I negotiated a $2.5 million line of credit with—guess who?—Bank of America. I didn't have a CFO at the time. I was so proud of the deal. I did it in 90 days. It's real tough for a tiny company like ours to get that kind of credit. Shortly after, the bank came down with all their problems. A VP came to visit, and I thought it was to congratulate a new customer. Instead, he told me that they're closing down their New England operations and that we should move our line of credit to another bank ASAP. All that effort went down the tubes, and I had to go out and do it all over again.

No matter how good the CFO is, venture capitalists and the banks want to spend a lot of time with the CEO. They want to really get to know how we get things done. My board tells me that the fact that I didn't have a CFO during two critical fund-raising periods was actually a good thing. We may have gotten funds easier and at a better price because they could spend more time with me.

We asked Hosage what he thought the critical skills on a management team were.

You've used the right word—the *team*. You need a good balance of marketing, development, financial, and manufacturing skills to make the company go. It used to be that technology was the predominant skill. High-tech has relied too heavily on the greatest and best "whiz bang." It got them money, but they didn't spend enough time on the broader aspects of the business.

At the beginning, you probably need a good technical product development resource. Next, you need a marketing resource. You have to translate a product into a utility that can be perceived and will be paid for by a good cut of your marketplace.

Manufacturing is next, you have to keep product cost down; it's a highly competitive world. You just can't have that much additional functionality and value without having competitive product cost. We had to take our manufacturing offshore in order to achieve that. And, boy, that wasn't an easy task for a small company to do.

I put the financial side last only because I was doing it for so long, and we satisfied the other needs first. Eventually, you must develop the principles of operational expense control and the disciplines of working well with the banks, stockholders, and investors. A CFO is really required to do all that effectively.

CASE STUDY: Great Grains

Often, the founding team in a venture will concentrate on the *whiz bang*, to use Hosage's words in the Davox Corporation case study. The team may ignore, among other things, the need for basic marketing and sales skills. Consider the following vignette, provided by the president of Great Grains (not the firm's real name) a wood processing and distribution firm in the Southeast part of the United States. Even though wood could hardly be called a high-tech product, we have seen enough evidence that this story could quite readily be applicable to many types of sales situations.

"We finally hired some salesmen of our own," the President of Great Grains told us. "The rep firms weren't working out. Three salesmen each wanted over $50,000 a year as a base salary, plus commissions. Their ages were 21, 42, and 57. After a while we found out that they weren't doing too much selling. Appointments weren't being kept. One was hanging around a local university library and reading. Another was showing up at softball practice. We finally implemented a sales lead tracking system to make sure that the salesmen were out selling."

The moral? There are many details that need attention when building a company. A complete set of management skills is needed in order to maximize your chances of success.

Two Case Studies: You Don't Need a Team for a One-Man Show

Throughout this chapter, we have stressed the importance of the management team and the value of a business plan in directing the energies of that team. In the two brief examples cited below, that logic is reversed. The names of the firms have been disguised because our comments could appear critical and that was not our intent.

CASE STUDY: CompuProcess

CompuProcess is a data processing services company in the Midwest. No business plan was written for the company, which was funded with the founder's money. No market analysis was performed, and the founder relied on the personal knowledge of the marketplace he had gained as a salesman for a mainframe manufacturer. There was no need to analyze the management team because, in his words, "There wasn't one. It's a one-man management team." Only sketchy financial analyses were performed.

Was CompuProcess handicapped by this founding history of the president wanting to maintain control? Well, the firm has been in business for 25 years, employs 66 people, and enjoys $16,000,000 in annual revenue.

CASE STUDY: Feedum, Inc.

Feedum is a food distribution firm in the Southwest, a family-owned business very much under the control of its president. No business plan was written for the company. When asked about a marketing plan, the founder said, "The marketing plan, if there was one, was formulated in my head and was not presented to anyone in writing. Our strategy was plain and simple—*sell* the product."

At first, no real financial analysis was done, because "the total income, developed from commissions, was not all that great. As our business grew, however, we did become a bit more regimented and now do a great deal of financial planning."

No analysis of the management team was done either because the founder felt that "it was more expedient to devote our time to selling and developing customers rather than making believe we were sufficiently sophisticated to analyze ourselves."

Feedum has now been in business for 20 years, has an annual income of $12,000,000, and employs 48 people.

The point of these two examples is simple. One purpose of a business plan is to help in pulling a management team together. If there is no management team, then a business plan may not be needed. This approach will work if the founder alone has all the needed skills for running the firm, finding the customers, selling the product, and servicing the customers after they have bought the product. Company founders such as these are rare, but they do exist.

4

Choosing the Audience for Your Plan

A banker is someone who won't lend you money until you can prove, without any doubt whatsoever, that you don't need it.

A Fundamental Law of Nature

What Is an Audience?

The term "audience" as used throughout this book refers to one or more people to whom you will present your business plan. This could include members of a venture capital firm, principals in a public accounting firm, investors, family members, customers, or competitors. They are people who can in some way help your firm or your founding management team achieve its objectives.

Why Worry About the Audience?

What do you expect your business plan to do for you? If your goals are like those of many other entrepreneurs, you anticipate funding, or gaining financial support for your business venture. Funding, of course, is a primary goal. However, support can come in other forms such as loan guarantees, joint marketing agreements, technical or managerial assistance, or agreements for the use of expensive equipment. Your business plan is a good route to seeking such assistance. In general, you will want to use the plan to persuade another person or firm to give you something of value. Your business plan is, therefore, a *marketing document.*

To be effective, you must tailor your marketing to your audience. By choosing carefully, you can find an audience that can provide you with the help you need; by tailoring your business plan to meet that audience's expectations, you can increase your chances of obtaining that help.

It is a myth to think that one does not have to *sell* a business plan. "Don't sell," the myth says. "Just present the facts in a sound way and the rest will take care of itself." Sadly, our experiences and those of many others have proven that "the rest" does not always take care of itself. Therefore, developing an approach to *marketing your business plan* is one of your crucial tasks.

Venture Capital Firms Are Not the Best First Audience

If you have been looking at the available literature on how to prepare an effective business plan, you probably have come across lists of venture capital firms, along with their addresses, phone numbers, and information on the types of investments they make. The conventional wisdom is that if you purchase a standard business plan outline, write a business plan using these guidelines, and send it to one of the firms listed in a venture capital directory, you will have a good shot at being funded.

Our information, on the other hand, goes against this conventional wisdom. We sent via direct mail 950 questionnaires to professional funding firms such as venture capital firms, small business investment companies (SBICs), and underwriters. We received 42 responses, or a 4.4 percent return, which is considered a very good response. We were able to use 30 of the 42 responses for detailed analyses of business plan volume and funding information.

We asked questions about the volume of business plans arriving every month and how many plans were funded each year. We asked whether the plans were unsolicited, referred, or generated internally. The results as outlined below may surprise you:

- The number of business plans arriving at each firm annually varied from 48 to 1,200, with an average of 486.8.
- The number of business plans funded each year ranged from 2 to 50, with an average of 9.2.
- The proportion of unsolicited, referred, and internally generated plans reported to us was as follows:

Unsolicited	55.2 percent
Referred	34.3 percent
Internal	10.4 percent

- The funding amounts per plan were reported as ranging from $75,000 to $10,000,000, with an average of $1,500,000.
- The total number of plans arriving at the 30 firms in our sample was estimated to be 14,604 per year.
- The total number of plans funded by the 30 firms in our sample was estimated to be 275 per year.

During in-depth interviews, we also asked representatives of ten selected firms how many of the funded plans were unsolicited. The percentage of unsolicited funded plans ranged from 1 to 3 percent.

Some computations are in order:

- The percentage of plans that were funded as a percentage of all plans arriving at the investor firms is $275/14,604 = 1.9$ percent.
- Using a median value of 2 percent, the number of funded plans that were unsolicited by the 30 firms in our sample is $0.02 \times 275 = 5.5$ plans per year.
- The percentage of unsolicited funded plans, based on all plans arriving at the 30 firms in our sample, is $5.5/14,604 = 0.039$ percent.

Our conclusions are as follows:

- If you send your unsolicited plan directly to a professional investment firm, the odds of obtaining funding are approximately 1 in 2,500.
- If your plan arrives at a professional investment firm through a trusted referral source, your odds of obtaining funding are approximately 1 in 50.

The next question we asked should be obvious: "How can the entrepreneur enlist a trusted referral source? Two answers we obtained spoke for all the others. According to Larry Mohr, General Partner of Mohr Davidow Ventures in Menlo Park, California, "Most venture capital firms want you to have a good law firm and a good accounting firm. The senior people in those firms know who the venture capitalists are and what they're looking for." Pat Hamner, Investment Associate with Capital Southwest Corporation in Dallas, Texas, added, "There are individuals out there who have brought us good plans, and we respect their views. We also take referrals from our own portfolio companies."

Venture capital firms were also mentioned as referral sources to other venture capital firms, but how do you get into the former without a referral?

The best referral sources are accounting firms, lawyers, people trusted by investors, and companies that have been funded before. Does this sound like a private club? You can get in, but it may not be easy.

Choose Your Audience Carefully

We have tried to show that your chances of success will improve if you do not send your plan directly to a professional investment firm. Selecting the right audience or appropriate referral source becomes critical, and that's what this chapter is about. How do you locate these trusted referral sources? Just ask. Find out the names of the accounting and legal firms that venture capital firms deal with. Then ask about the companies they've funded. Get the name of a successful local company that has been funded, and ask about the firm that funded it as well as the accounting and legal firms they retain.

You may wonder if professional investment firms will give you information of this nature. In gathering research for this book, we called a number of firms and asked them many questions. Roughly half of the firms queried provided us with valuable answers.

Will the referral sources, such as accounting and legal firms, you contact talk with you? The answer is probably "yes." Our experience has been that principals in the small business divisions of accounting firms will always talk with you. Frankly, they hope you will retain them as auditors once you start your company. As for lawyers, all it takes is money. We found that we could retain a lawyer any time we wanted to.

We also learned that founders of newly funded companies were more than willing to talk with us, so long as their companies were healthy and growing. Many successful founders we spoke with felt an obligation to help people just getting started.

You can lose time, energy, and money with a bad choice of audience, as the following case study explains.

CASE STUDY: The Wide World Software Company

Four founders formed a fledgling software company whose fictionalized name is Wide World Software. Among them, the management team had accumulated 75 years of management and technical experience. Wide World's product was an applications software package for use by large data processing installations. The software directly and successfully solved a recognized problem within the market segment being addressed—that is, the clear identification of costs and the modelling of alternative methods and technologies within the data processing environment. Customer interviews showed that a need for this product existed, and literature searches showed that competitors were building toward this capability although no direct competitor existed.

Wide World had been selling single units of the software package as part of a family of products, with dozens of successful installations completed. Its next task was to begin mass marketing of the product and installations in larger numbers. The founders of Wide World decided to prepare their first business plan and approach outside funding sources.

After several meetings and many long-distance telephone calls (the founders lived 2,000 miles apart) the basic steps of a business plan were agreed upon and a plan was prepared. The founders were excited because this was the culmination of many years of hard work in developing and proving Wide World Software Company's products.

To begin, the founders contacted many venture capital firms and most of the Big Eight accounting firms. The venture capital firms did not want to be bothered and would not even comment until they could read a finished business plan. Six of the accounting firms responded. Of these, three had well-written materials on business planning services available, were willing to spend time talking to the founders, and had qualified people in the local office. (The kind of help you will be able to get from an accounting firm will depend very heavily on the people in that firm's local office.)

The founders sought advice from the three accounting firms as to what was expected in a business plan. These three firms offered their standard business plan outlines, and their principals took time to discuss the project with Wide World's founders and how the plan should be written. The founders used these firms' outlines and advice to structure and prepare their business plan.

Six weeks of intensive work spread out over a three-month period were needed to complete the plan, with the effort sandwiched between ongoing work activities and the Christmas holidays. Two major versions of the plan were produced, and the "Executive Summary" was heavily rewritten four times. The completed plan showed a need for $1.5 million in funding and projected a return on an investment of roughly 40 percent.

Principals in the three accounting firms reviewed the plan and circulated some of the details to other members in their organizations. Not one of them, however, was able to match Wide World with venture capital clients they were working with at that time. The founders, however, identified six venture capital firms that claimed to want software investment opportunities. Initial contacts were made by phone, and copies of the plan were mailed to a specific person in each firm.

The results were disappointing because all six firms rejected the business plan. Curiously, there was no consistent reason given for the rejection, as shown on the responses below:

Firm 1: You have a product, but no management team.

Firm 2: You have a management team and a product, but your marketing plan isn't firm enough.

Firm 3: You're not asking for enough money. It's not worth it.

Firm 4: I'm investing my own money and I don't invest in software. *(According to the office staff, the firm did invest in software.)*

Firm 5: We lost the plan. Would you mind sending us another copy?

Firm 6: We don't accept plans over the transom. *(The person responding had asked to see the plan.)*

In four of the six firms the plan was read by people who had recently received their MBAs and who had no other business experience. In no case would a firm offer constructive criticism, and several turndowns were arrogantly phrased: "We're not going to train you," or "We don't have to explain why we rejected the plan."

Wide World's founders were discouraged and for several weeks considered scrapping the venture. However, a post-mortem evaluation revealed some of the reasons for the failure:

- The founders had relied too heavily on the published descriptions of the special interests of each of the firms involved.
- The founders had sent their plans only to firms indicating a preference for software ventures. Further, the founders learned that software investments had been strongly discouraged at a recent venture capital

conference. Subsequent questions to each of the six firms revealed that they all knew of the recommendation of that conference. Thus, each venture capital firm had decided to curtail its investment in software before asking to see and review Wide World's plan.

- None of the firms had voluntarily informed Wide World's founders of this significant external factor, which contributed to the rejection of the business plan.

The post-mortem analysis also helped the founders understand that they had chosen their audience incorrectly. So, Wide World expanded its search, looking at large software firms with compatible product lines. One such firm the founders contacted asked for more and more information, with different views on the market and the product. After several iterations, the founders realized that they were being used to provide free market research, and they broke off the discussions.

One firm was finally identified, however, which seemed to benefit from an association with Wide World's product. The business plan was revised and reviewed with that firm, and serious negotiations for funding and other support finally began.

The Lessons to Be Learned

Initially, the business plan must make contacts for you. It must get you through the screening process, win you referrals, and convince potential investors that you, your product, and your management team are worth the expense and effort that a more detailed evaluation will require. While making that initial contact, your plan is essentially considered a marketing document.

After the initial contact has blossomed into a serious interest, a full-scale analysis of your plan will follow. At this point the business plan must communicate clearly what you need and what you are offering in return. You can approach several different audiences with the same plan. Each audience will have its own objectives, concerns, and information needs. Choosing and understanding the right audience is crucial to the success of the business plan.

Time is both a critical resource and an enemy for the entrepreneur. If you truly have a hot idea, it is likely that others have spotted the same idea and are working on a business plan similar to yours. Therefore, choose your audience wisely and prepare your business plan carefully, minimizing the number of false starts you make before arriving at a plan that will be reviewed and, hopefully, accepted.

The energy and spirit of the founders are other critical resources for the entrepreneur. You will invest evenings, weekends, and more than a small amount of money into the preparation of a business plan. If the business plan fails, you will have wasted not only time and money but also a bit of the spirit of your founding team. You will soon discover that *spirit* is the hardest asset of all to replace.

Expect a few unpleasant responses from the people you contact. Whatever the reason—be it status, power, ego, or just plain incompetence—you can count on at least one nasty response. Not everyone will respond negatively, of course, but when they do, the impact on you can be significant if you are not psychologically prepared to bounce back.

How Does the Audience Affect the Business Plan?

In general, the basic outline of any business plan will remain the same as that which will be suggested in Chapter 6. The emphasis placed on each section and, to some extent, the detail included will vary depending on the audience you have selected for the business plan. A venture capital firm would have different objectives for investing in your business plan than, say, a company with a complementary product line.

Potential Audiences for Your Business Plan

Listed below are only some of the many potential audiences for your business plan. They are cited in approximately the same order of frequency with which they were mentioned by the 78 company founders responding to our questionnaires.

Founders and their families
Banks
Other firms with a related product
Existing or potential customers
Your current employer
Sophisticated individual investors
Your employees
Venture capital firms
Small business investment companies
Underwriters
Limited partnerships

Other audiences worth mentioning are the Small Business Administration and that organization's Small Business Innovation Research Grants.

Consider the Agenda of Your Audience

Each audience will be interested in specific aspects of your business plan. Their interests will affect the way the finished plan is written. Therefore, it pays to review each of the various audience possibilities while the plan is in the rough draft stage. This will allow the specific concerns and interests of the chosen audience to be included in the finished product.

One critic describes this approach as *manipulation*. We disagree. A competent firm or investor will soon discover problems with your plan. No amount of tailoring of the plan will prevent that from happening. (Take it on faith that you do not want to deal with incompetent individuals and investment firms.) However, you can and should do everything possible to present your plan clearly and highlight those areas that are important to the audience you have chosen.

Each of the potential audiences will be described in some detail in the following sections, along with ways in which the basic business plan should be modified to meet that audience's needs.

Founders and Their Families

Virtually all of the people responding to our questionnaires who were original founders of their firms invested their own money to get started. Those who did not invest cash used their homes as collateral for a loan. Some founders did both.

Many founders did minimal business planning when they started, sometimes planning only for cash flow and expenses. A small number did no planning at all. (See the section "You Don't Need a Team for a One-Man Show" at the end of Chapter 3.)

Some people think they need not bother with a business plan if they are using their own money as an initial investment. We do not agree with this concept because the business planning process forces prospective founders to examine and question every aspect of their businesses. Your chances of success, or of greater success, will be markedly improved by following through on the business planning process. Our comments in the sections below on dealing with sophisticated individual investors will also apply to dealing with your own management team and their families.

Banks

Many of the founder respondents to our questionnaires indicated that they had either started their companies with a bank loan or obtained a loan or line of credit at some other point in their companies' existence.

It is not possible to get a bank loan without collateral and a credible means of repaying the debt. *Collateral* such as your house, stocks and bonds (as long as their value does not fall), or cash are considered good assets for backing a bank loan. Capital equipment also can be used with some banks. In a few rare cases, a signed contract specifying unconditional payments can be used as collateral if those payments are assigned to the bank.

You should understand how banks operate. An individual banker rarely makes a loan to an individual entrepreneur. The loan application usually is submitted to a review committee, which tests the soundness of the deal. If the bank can accommodate a particular loan, and if it looks like a sound investment, the bank will approve it.

Banks are also under constant scrutiny and cannot afford to carry many risky loans in their portfolios. If a bank's internal or external auditors, or bank examiners, find too many risky loans, the bank can be penalized or, in extreme cases, closed down.

Do not overlook the "lemming effect" when dealing with banks. Once a prominent bank starts to make profitable loans in one industry, other banks flock to make similar loans. If you are not in a favored industry, you will have a harder selling job ahead of you.

If you have a business plan that is marginally risky, you may be able to find a bank that will listen to your request for funds. Banks usually have a limited amount of money that can be invested in risky ventures, for which they will probably charge higher interest. You may be able to win access to these discretionary funds. This means that you may have to contact many banks to find one that will help you.

Remember, too, that your venture might fail. If you play "you-bet-your-house" by using your home as collateral, you will receive no sympathy from the bank if foreclosure proceedings are in order.

Several variations on bank loans may be of some use. For example, by using capital equipment as collateral, it is possible to arrange for a leasing company to provide funds for the equipment. Or, by using signed purchase contracts as collateral, a factoring firm may give you advance cash for your accounts receivable. Both of these options are likely to be more expensive than bank loans, however, because leasing companies and factoring firms usually obtain their money from banks.

A bank studying your business plan will be interested mainly in the financial statements of your firm and, if the firm is small, its principals. It will want to know about the firm's history, the principals, and their backgrounds. A bank also will want to know what assets you can pledge to guarantee the debt. Most of all, it will want credible proof that you are able to repay the debt.

A standard business plan with emphasis on the above topics can help a bank analyze the future prospects of your firm and meet other bank information needs.

Other Firms with a Related Product

Two types of firms fall into this category: firms with *competing* products and firms with *complementary* products.

A firm with a competing project may be interested in your firm or product because it either perceives your product to be an improvement over its own or it fears that you will take away its customers. A competitor may become convinced that it is in its best interest to buy out your product or firm.

Also, government regulations may cause a competitor to be interested in your firm. We learned of a case in which a firm bidding on government contracts lost because it was the only supplier of a particular product. The firm invested in a competitor, and both firms subsequently bid on a contract. (The other firm won.)

A firm with a complementary product line may view your product as a potential enhancement of its own offerings. To this kind of firm you represent an opportunity to add a product without heavy investment in R&D, thereby eliminating the usual time lag involved in research.

In both of these cases, the firms will be interested in the potential impact of your product or firm on their markets. They will:

- Place an emphasis on the product and on your analysis of the market.
- Want to know what is needed to sell and service the product because their personnel may end up supporting it.
- Want to know about any special functions or skills available in your firm, which could be involved through an ongoing arrangement with them. For example, if planning the development of future products is at issue, the qualifications of your R&D staff will be of interest.
- Want to independently analyze the market and the price for the product, and determine whether the money you want is practical for them.

When preparing a business plan for this type of audience, emphasize portions of the plan that highlight these activities. The financial operation of your firm and your plans for future expenditures are important only if they relate to the deal being discussed. (The audience may want to know that you are, or will be, financially secure under the proposed arrangement.) The main factor here is how you can help the firm to which you are presenting the plan. You can probably assume a somewhat higher degree of sophistication on the part of your audience than is usually the case.

Members of another firm in the same industry as your own will be able to understand—and may expect to see—more detailed and technical product specifications than those from outside the industry. With this type of audience, your market analysis can and should be especially thorough and detailed, because it is likely that a complementary firm will be quite knowledgeable about the market. Keep in mind that this audience will have its own market information, however, so before launching into a lengthy study, you may want to ask the company for the amount of detail they require.

Existing or Potential Customers

If customers are interested in your product and like it enough, they may want to invest in your company. (Remember Victor Kiam? "I bought the Remington Electric Shaver, and I liked it so much, I bought the company.")

Go back and reread the Davox Corporation Case Study at the end of Chapter 3. The firm signed on two of its major corporate customers as investors, selling them shares in the firm. Davox had an existing product, and the sequence of deals is clear. Davox first interested the firms in its products and agreed on terms for a sale. Then the discussions about investment were held. (It would probably be a mistake to try to reverse the order if your product is already in existence.)

It has become increasingly common in the computer software industry to rely on customer funding for new product development. For example, ANACOMP, a large software venture, was funded by potential customers—in this case, banks—joined in a limited partnership format. For several reasons, the firm is having some well-publicized problems, but the funding method appears to be sound. There is little to prevent this method of customer funding from working in many other industries as well.

The basic approach is to locate a group of customers who would be interested in your product if it were available. Once you identify this audience, you must describe what you are offering and the kind of help you are seeking.

Assistance from existing or potential customers can come in many forms. The simplest way is to have customers pay for the product in advance. This audience also may participate in the design and testing of the product, using its industry and working knowledge to reduce your R&D costs. Here are some ways in which your customers can assist you:

- Offer laboratories in which their operation becomes a data source for studies you conduct.
- Participate in marketing research activities such as focus groups.
- Allow you to use expensive equipment such as computers or chemical laboratories.
- Serve as publicized reference accounts once your product has been put into use.
- Provide funding or its equivalent to help get your product off the ground.

An existing business may want to help you for some of the following reasons:

- To participate in a state-of-the-art development project.
- To gain a competitive advantage because these participants in the venture would have access to your product before the rest of the industry.
- To have a say in the design of the product, ensuring that it comes closer to meeting their needs.
- To respond to a good, old-fashioned discount on the product in return for advance payment.

Whatever the reason, you may rest assured that firms electing to help will do so out of self-interest. They might also want a small amount of equity in your venture in return for their help.

The search process for a compatible firm to serve as a partner in a venture can be easier on company founders than dealing with investors. On the whole, when engaged in discussions with investment groups, we continually ran into problems with ego, unprofessional conduct, and just plain rudeness, which can be frustrating, demeaning, and draining. In dealing with corporate business firms, however, we encountered less of this behavior. The change was very welcome indeed.

An audience comprising compatible firms will be very interested in your product, its relationship to competitive products, and what it can do for them. Members of these firms also need to find out what kind of help you need.

When presenting a business plan to this audience, you should de-emphasize the financial portions of your business plan and perhaps consider not sharing that information at all. Keep in mind that you are asking this audience to participate as *customers*, not as investors. The value they receive will be the product itself. If you are working with employees rather than owners of the firm, the details of your hoped-for financial success might trigger some resentment.

When and if you begin talking about investment, the considerations listed under "Sophisticated Individual Investors," in a following section, will also apply here.

Your Current Employer

There are two ways to have your employer fund your product idea: as a spinoff company and as an employee.

Like many people with new product ideas, it is likely that you are working for someone else. This gives you the option of presenting the product idea to your employer for funding and development. Once presented, this idea can be developed in-house or spun off into a new company.

Appealing to the audience of "current employer" may simplify the job of presenting a product idea because the firm probably has its own business planning specialists, and a formal business plan may not be necessary until after the product concept is sold.

There are several reasons why your current firm may assist you in a spinoff. If you are a capable product development person, with an ability to come up with new product ideas, you are probably considered as an asset to your employer. As a first priority, the firm would want to keep you as an employee. On the other hand, when faced with losing an asset such as you, the firm may consider you as a spinoff. Employers are sometimes interested in investing in spinoff, however, because they can exert more control and benefit from their investment in you. Without their participation, your product may become a competitor to theirs. Keep in mind though that it may be more feasible and less expensive to develop a product through a smaller, newer firm than within the existing structure of an already established firm.

This is the one audience with whom the product idea itself may be enough to generate interest and begin the funding process because it knows the market and the competition; therefore, these topics do not have to be written up in the business plan. Also, the company knows you, so your background and skills need not be documented.

Although this seems like a simple path to follow, there are pitfalls with this audience. For example, if part of your job function is to create product ideas, or if the firm assumes that is the case, the company may believe that it already owns the product and all profits from it. As a result, you may have to be satisfied with a raise or a bonus. If you are in a position to negotiate a better deal, such as a portion of the net profit from the product or perhaps some equity in the firm, so much the better. However, as an employee, your leverage may be limited—particularly if you have signed an employment contract in which you signed over the rights to anything you create and develop.

If the contract is loosely worded, signing over the rights may appear to extend to *anything* you develop, whether or not it is developed on company time. If you have not signed anything but the firm has a written policy that states that anything you develop is theirs, this may pose a problem also.

The safest way to deal with this type of situation is to present the idea to your employer. If the principals in the firm are not interested in the product, ask them to sign a statement to that effect. Also be sure to develop the product on your own time, using your own resources, and be prepared to prove it. If you use the firm's facilities, it may believe it has a claim on profits from the product. Here are a few suggestions for this approach:

- If you have signed an employment contract, or if your firm has written policies dealing with this topic, take the relevant materials to an attorney and determine what your position is. You should be aware of this information before divulging your ideas.
- Whether or not you have signed an employment contract, approach your firm with the idea. By practicing full disclosure, you will avoid later accusations of "we didn't know."
- If the firm is interested, ask that arrangements such as bonus payments and royalties be considered. Such terms may leave them with enough profit to be interested in funding the venture while directing some of the revenue to you.
- If the firm isn't interested in developing the product, you may decide to take the giant step of asking the principals in the company if they would provide funding for a new company that would be started by you and your co-founders. In this instance, the firm would develop the product and set up a separate division to pro-

duce it, with you as the division president holding significant equity. The funding could be in either debt or equity form, as agreed upon by both parties.

This is the easiest, least aggressive way to get your product idea funded. However, it is also most likely to be the least profitable approach for you.

In most cases, in order to realize the full potential of a good new business opportunity, though, you will probably have to leave the company and form your own startup.

Sophisticated Individual Investors

You may know of people who are interested in investing in your product or company. If they are sophisticated investors, the reasons for their investment will be similar to those of a venture capital firm. This audience is looking for more return than that available through other investments. It also may be looking for a specific type or form of investment to meet its own tax or cash flow needs.

You are probably on safe ground when dealing with knowledgeable and sophisticated investors because these people are likely to analyze the potential investment very carefully and discover any obvious problems or flaws.

In fact, it is to your advantage to uncover any problems before you receive funding, in order to avoid possible lawsuits by investors wanting to recover their money. The due diligence process, used by professional investors to research business plans before investments are made, is actually a good tool for you as well because it can reveal weaknesses in your plan. Their correction will improve your chances of success.

Dealing with unsophisticated investors, especially if they are family or friends, may seem appealing. Many of the founders who responded to our questionnaires told us they had started their firms with family money. You can take Aunt Mary's money, for example, and bypass all the due diligence steps that normally precede funding through conventional means. But, a word of caution to founders with rich relatives: Nothing can break up a friendship or a family relationship faster than the loss of money. The due diligence steps that you may bypass in this way are intended to ensure that your venture can and will succeed. When you sidestep this analysis, you may not discover problems that could cause you to fail until it is too late. Thus, an easy path to funding might become the fast track to failure and the relationship involved will be a definite casualty.

We offer two suggestions for dealing with individual investors.

First, ensure that there is full disclosure of everything that even remotely relates to an investment in your business plan. All risks, no matter
how small, should be spelled out, *in writing*, in your business plan. Phrases
such as "This plan is based on our assumptions" (include a detailed list of
those assumptions), "Achievement of the financial targets is dependent on
crop production in the Midwest," "There is no guarantee that we are
correct," and "The investors may never get their money back" should be
scattered through the text. An attorney can help you with the phrasing.
Make sure the investors are aware of the risks, and have them sign a
statement to that effect. For examples of this type of disclosure, read a
prospectus for a public stock offering.

Second, we suggest bypassing a wealthy relative in favor of a "sophisticated investor." This is a legal term, requiring that the investor have
a specific net worth and that he or she meet certain other requirements.
Again, an attorney can help you with the details. A sophisticated investor
may be experienced in the industry you are working in, which will help
him or her to understand the risks involved. It will also make a certain
amount of knowledge available to you in setting up your venture, which
can only help insure your success. If you absolutely must take funding
from an unsophisticated investor, at least retain a consultant who can
perform the due diligence steps that would normally be performed for
other types of investors. In the long run, it will pay you to take this advice
seriously.

The sophisticated investor will be interested in the information in the
traditional business plan, with emphasis on the risks of the investment
and its potential return.

Be careful about how you search for investors. Advertisements appear daily in business journals, which ask, in one way or another, for
investors. State government agencies and the Securities and Exchange
Commission require that companies go through the registration process
before advertising for the sale of a security. The bureaucrats will usually
accept proof of a prior relationship between a firm and an investor as an
acceptable excuse for talking with a prospective investor about a particular opportunity. Consult a competent attorney before searching for investors, as this will affect the specific wording in your business plan.

When working with an individual investor, do not allow the relationship to become casual. Surround yourself with documentation, keeping
track of each and every step in the process—beginning with the business
plan, including full disclosures of all the risks involved. If business problems develop, be the first to identify and report them. Maintain a formal
communication with the investor, in writing—even if it involves family

members or close friends. At first, this may seem silly, but you will not be sorry if the venture fails.

A note about working with attorneys. We have indicated several times that certain situations call for professional advice. In our opinion, if you are running a company, starting a venture, or writing a business plan, you should do a great deal of homework toward solving your own problems. After you have a good understanding of the issues involved, *then* look for an attorney. Find one who:

- Will work with you and not be insulted that you are trying to understand the law involved.
- Will seek creative solutions and help implement them.
- Will charge a reasonable fee for the amount of work he or she puts into a project.

We have, sadly enough, had some bad experiences with attorneys. They are not all bad, we know. Our sampling method must have been biased.

In our experience, it is best to have an attorney handle specific issues such as agreements, licenses, trademarks, copyrights, or the legal or financial structure of the company. A good attorney is hard to find and deserves your loyalty. If you select one who is both a creative thinker and an implementer of solutions, then stick with him or her. We continue to retain an attorney who has moved to another state since we first employed him.

Your Employees

A business plan may be developed as an internal document that tells your employees where you expect the firm to be in the next several years, and how they might help the firm get there.

At the end of this chapter, you will find a case study of the Nor-Cote Chemical Company. In this instance, the firm sold stock to and obtained loans from its employees. The interesting approach was unique among the responses we received to our questionnaires because it suggests a fairly novel method of financing your company's growth while offering equity to your employees in exchange for capital.

There are several benefits of having your own employees as an audience for your business plan. The employees become shareholders, are given financial information about the firm, and feel that they have a stake in the firm's success. As the Nor-Cote Case Study shows, employees can

develop good attitudes toward the customers and toward solving problems. The only disadvantage that comes to mind is the dilution of the
original equity in the firm and the potential loss of control. These things
can be handled by careful planning, of course, and by placing limits on
the amount of stock that employees can purchase.

If you wish to use a business plan to seek funding from your employees, you will find that they are going to be interested in much the same
information as sophisticated investors.

Referral Sources

For referrals to venture capital (VC) firms and other investors, present a business plan following the standard outline to accounting firms,
law firms, and companies that have received funding from these organizations.

There is no easy way to obtain the names of referrals to professional
investment firms. The VC firms will either tell you, or not tell you, which
companies they have funded. The funded firms will either tell you, or not
tell you, which VC firms funded them. Rest assured that the accounting
and law firms will not tell you who their clients are. Here are a few
suggestions for finding the information you are seeking:

- A visit to the library may yield some newspaper or magazine articles that describe a firm and its funders.
- Get out your phone book and call your former working associates,
  college friends, or distant family members. Someone will refer you
  to a helpful source.
- Locate local venture capital clubs or local networking groups and
  attend their meetings. The accounting firms or venture capital companies in your area will probably know of these groups and how to
  contact them. These groups are comprised of firms looking for money
  and of firms looking for places to invest. Through discussions and
  presentations at these meetings, you can learn about other firms seeking investors and their funders.

Venture Capital Firms

Venture capital firms are collections of individuals with a responsibility for investing money. Most VC firms invest money belonging to
groups of individuals or to large institutional funds, banks, or corporations. Very few of these organizations use their own money. If a VC firm
invests in a poor venture, it can lose millions of dollars. If it can be proven

that the money was lost through incompetence or neglect, the VC firm will probably be sued by the people whose money it invested, which makes these professional investors a little wary.

VC firms tend to be interested in specific industries in which they have experience and knowledge, and which seem to be good for investors. They may also prefer to invest their money in specific product types within those industries.

Expect VC firms to be strongly influenced by current trends. When specific industries and products appear in the trade press and catch the professional investors' eye, it is difficult to get them to look at any other type of opportunities.

They usually expect a higher return than is available from other forms of investment. In fact, the investment return sought by VC firms has been described by some observers as unrealistically high. (On the questionnaires returned to us by professional investors, those who provided data said they looked forward to returns ranging from 2 to 5 times their original investments.)

VC firms expect many of their investments to fail. The ones that succeed—estimated by those who answered our questionnaire as approximately one in five—must make very high rates of return to keep the averages for their firms at acceptable levels. This amounts to approximately 30 to 40 percent annual return as reported by the firms we interviewed, thereby causing VC firms to look for explosive opportunities. A mere "good" investment may not stand a chance.

(Rhetorical question: What would happen if the VC firms looked for four out of five of their ventures to succeed at a 50 percent return rather than one out of five at 500 percent, return on investment?)

It is to your advantage to interview several VC firms. The people employed by these firms have varying degrees of experience and education. Look for a firm whose staff has 10 to 15 years of working experience in your industry, and scrutinize the financial, marketing, legal, and accounting expertise within the firm. It is common for VC firms to employ young MBA graduates to screen business plans. These staffers follow guidelines set by the firm, and it may be difficult to get your plan through their screening.

The skills and experience of the senior members of a VC firm can work to your advantage. If a principal in a firm reviews your plan and thinks you should be rejected, his or her analysis of the reasons why will prove invaluable to you when deciding what to do next. If you are lucky and your plan is funded, experienced senior staffers in the firm can provide skills that your management team may not possess.

Interview a VC firm before submitting your plan to determine its screening guidelines, and learn what experience and skills the firm has available to support your specific product and industry. You can also learn about that firm's track record in aiding ventures similar to yours.

Occasionally, you will receive adverse reactions when you ask for information, especially from small VC firms. Usually, it is the people asking for money who are examined in excruciating, sometimes painful detail, and it is the VC firms that ask the questions. Their negative reactions may show up in different ways. For example, firm representatives may not return your phone calls, may lecture you on the phone, or may simply reject your business plan. If any of these happen, keep looking for a firm that will respond to your questions and provide you with the references you need.

In general, most VC firms are likely to use the same approach when evaluating a business plan. Based on the responses to our questionnaires as well as a number of selected interviews, these companies are primarily interested in:

How the plan reached them, whether by referral or directly
The management team
How much investment is required
When and how they can get their investment out
The product and its market
The marketing, operating, and financial plans

VC firms tend to be most interested in opportunities that have the potential for a big ticket buyout, such as a public offering. Therefore, it is useful to understand where you and your product stand with respect to a public offering. A $10M to $15M guideline is often used as a minimum annual revenue in order for a company to be considered in a public offering. For a startup, achieving this level of revenue could take from five to seven years or more. Rarely is a business taken public earlier in the life of the firm.

VC firms also may have a preference as to the way an investment is made. Some will invest "seed money" in startups, others prefer to wait until the later rounds of funding, while still others have a minimum amount of investment that they will consider.

You probably will not personally receive any initial cash from a VC deal. You may have spent three, five, or even seven years bringing your product opportunity to the point at which you seek funding from a VC. But, to the VC firm the clock starts on the day your business plan comes into the office. Nothing prior to that time has any value. And, it will take some tricky negotiating to be compensated at all for the time and expense you have put into the effort. Professional investors feel that they are only losing their money by paying the founders a fee of any kind.

A VC firm may take equity in your venture and demand control. The amount of equity will depend on the stage your venture is in, the risk involved, and the amount of investment it is called on to make. The amount of equity and the type of control or involvement demanded will vary from firm to firm.

In general, a VC firm does not want to run your company. It wants to make sure that a good management team and business plan are in place and that the management team will follow the business plan. If things go sour, however, the firm may get heavily involved. It may simply volunteer its management skills, or if it is in control, may replace members of your management team or force you to sell your interest in your own company. The VC firm will do whatever it can to protect its investment. Therefore, you should weigh these factors when electing to proceed along the VC route. Davox's Daniel Hosage offered this comment during his interview.

> Don't ever forget that the investor sitting on your board of directors may have investments in ten companies. He only needs two of them to succeed. If yours is one of them, fine. But expect him to do whatever he has to do to protect his investment and cut his losses.

You should ask detailed questions about these topics of the VC firms you are trying to work with. While the firms may be willing to provide only limited information without seeing a fully completed business plan, any information you obtain will help you in two ways.

First, it will help you locate one or more firms that have the experience and skills to help you in your venture.
Second, it will help you identify those things that are important to a particular firm and the criteria by which your plan will be judged.

These can help you emphasize the appropriate factors and areas as the business plan is completed.

The following checklist of questions may help you in interviewing the VC firms you are interested in working with:

What industry and product areas do you specialize in? The firms may answer that this does not matter. However, persist in asking until they tell you what types of companies they have been funding for, say, the past two years. The larger firms may have a few areas of specialization whereas the smaller ones may restrict their activities to just one area.

What rounds of funding are you interested in? They may or may not answer this question, saying that they want to see details of your opportunity first. Again, keep asking until you get an answer.

What are your criteria for evaluating a business plan? Although the answer to this question should be relatively easy to obtain, you may have to describe your business plan a little to maintain the interest of the person you have called.

Who will evaluate my business plan? What level of related experience does he or she have?

How many people are there in your firm? Find out the type of support that could be available for a venture that the VC firm might fund.

Have you funded a comparable venture? Ask for a list of names of people you would like to contact.

Do you take equity? Find out how much and how that proportion is determined.

Under what conditions do you want control?

What methods do you prefer for getting your investment and profit out of a venture?

You may not receive answers to all of the questions above, but the answers you do get should prove useful in choosing a firm—or in deciding on an alternative approach.

The standard business plan outline presented in Chapter 6 is intended for the VC firm audience. It will not be necessary to tailor your business plan unless you pick up specific information during your interviews with the VC firms.

Small Business Investment Corporations

A small business investment corporation (SBIC) is an organization of investors licensed through the SBA to provide funding for small businesses. SBIC funds may be used either for startups or for the expansion of existing operations. Like VC firms, SBICs may have specific industry or product preferences. Obtaining a license as an SBIC represents leverage for the investors. For each $1 invested by an SBIC, the SBA invests $3. Thus, to fund a $1 million venture, the investors need only put up $250,000. In return for their investment, the SBIC takes equity in firms it funds. This gives the SBIC some measure of control over the venture and provides a method of getting its money out at a later date.

The SBIC often provides management consulting to the firms it funds, although it does so for a fee. You should ask enough questions to understand what types of expertise the SBIC can offer and the experience of the personnel who will be involved. If you are going to pay for SBIC services, you should know what you are buying.

Some sources tell us that approaching an SBIC can mean a lengthy process of qualifying for funds and significant reporting requirements. The one SBIC that we interviewed, however, said that this is untrue. While the SBIC itself has quite a substantial reporting burden to the SBA, the borrowers do not.

During one interview, an SBIC principal said: "We don't impose a heavy reporting requirement on firms we fund. We ask to see the normal monthly, quarterly, and annual financial reports, and there may be specific analyses we ask for if it looks like there may be a problem. There are a few papers to sign for the SBA, such as an equal opportunity statement. Our paperwork load with the SBA, however, is much greater, but we never pass that on to our clients."

Each SBIC generally has its own guidelines, which are used to qualify a company for assistance. Some might suggest, for example, that a company register a certain net worth for three consecutive years or that there be a recommended minimum number of employees. The SBICs themselves, and the small business advisory practice within major public accounting firms, can provide information on these guidelines.

As the author of a business plan, you must be prepared for a fairly rigorous evaluation process if you present it to a SBIC, providing more written documentation on the initial contact about your product and yourself than for a VC firm.

Again, locate several of these firms and interview them to determine whether you want to work with them. Addresses and phone numbers are listed in any one of the popular venture capital guides, and the SBA office in your region can refer you to the SBIC nearest you. Use the questions under "Venture Capital Firms" above as a starting point, and supplement them with this line of questioning:

> *Do you provide management assistance?* If so, is it free or is a fee charged? What are the fees?
> *Who are the people providing the service?* What are their backgrounds?
> *What projects has your organization worked on?*

The standard business plan outline should be used.

Underwriters

We mention underwriters primarily because they were included in the mailing of questionnaires we sent out. Three underwriting firms responded. In our view, underwriters are not a feasible avenue for the average startup and are useful only to those few existing firms that can qualify for a public offering.

An underwriter can be an investment banker or a broker that is willing to underwrite the risks of a public offering of any type of securities. If your firm issued bonds, for example, an underwriter would purchase the issue from you, usually at a slight discount. The underwriting firm would then distribute and resell the securities at the market price. If the price falls between the time of issue and the time of sale, the underwriter can suffer a substantial loss because it is underwriting the risk of that loss.

Distribution of the securities for sale is critical. If an investment banker is the underwriter for an issue, it is not uncommon to see brokerage firms involved in the project. Some of the larger brokerage firms combine both investment banking and brokerage functions.

The basic steps for underwriting an issue are:

1. A pre-underwriting conference is held with the issuing firm and the investment banker to discuss the amount of money needed, the type of security to be issued, and the terms of an agreement.
2. The issuing firm's officers and board of directors approve the agreement.
3. An initial agreement is entered into with the investment banker that a securities offering—called a "flotation"—will be made.
4. An accounting firm is engaged to audit the issuing firm. A law firm is engaged to interpret legal aspects of the flotation. The underwriter does an exhaustive study of the issuing firm's prospects. The underwriter's technical staff may analyze the offering in detail.
5. The investment banker and the issuing firm enter a final underwriting agreement. All terms of the issue are included except the price of the security.
6. A registration statement is filed with the SEC. During a 20-day time period, which can be made shorter or longer at the SEC's option, the registration statement is analyzed for omissions or misrepresentations. The securities cannot be sold during this time, but a preliminary prospectus can be issued, without the price of the security.
7. When the SEC releases the issue, the price of the security is set.

The issuer naturally wants the price to be as high as possible, while the underwriter tries to keep it low. The price of the issuing firm's other securities, or of similar securities issued by other firms, is used to determine the price of the new securities.

The cost of underwriting can be very high. Weston and Brigham studied the costs of underwriting for issues of securities during the period from 1971 to 1975,* showing that the percentage of the amount raised varies by the size of the issue:

Size of Issue ($000)	Total Cost as a Percentage of Proceeds
Under $500	n/a
$500–$999	13.74
$1,000–$1,999	15.29
$2,000–$4,999	9.47
$5,000–$9,999	7.03
$10,000–$19,999	5.55
$20,000–$50,000	4.67

Other sources told us that costs for issues of under $500,000 can amount to 25 percent of the proceeds. Expenses of the issue, such as accounting and legal fees, may have to be paid in advance, making this a very expensive source of obtaining money.

The standard business plan outline should be followed.

Small Business Innovation Research Grants

The small Business Administration can tell you about the Small Business Innovation Research Grant program. Each major federal government agency publishes a list of projects under this program each year. The list contains the type of research or product needed and the closing date for bids on that project. The funding agency will provide specifics about each project and will process the proposals submitted. If your proposal is selected, you can receive up to $50,000 in first phase funding. If second phase funding is approved, you can receive up to $500,000.

If the product has commercial applicability, *you retain the rights to the product.*

*See J. Fred Weston and Eugene F. Brigham's *Managerial Finance* (Hinsdale, Ill.: Dryden Press, 1981), p. 732.

This sounds so good that it seems it cannot possibly be a government program. Sure enough, at this writing, the SBA is being discussed as a possible "sunset" candidate agency whose funding may soon be eliminated.

Limited Partnerships

A limited partnership is a formal method of gathering funds from one or more investors and placing them in a security. They are mentioned here, not because they are a primary audience for business plans but because they may offer a solution to some of the problems you are trying to solve by looking for a suitable audience.

The operation of a limited partnership is described by John L. Kearney, an attorney in Solana Beach, California.

> A limited partnership is an association of one or more general partners and one or more limited partners to carry on, as co-owners, a business for profit. A limited partner is an investor who is given limited liability as long as he or she does not participate in control of the partnership's business. The affairs of the partnership are managed by the general partners.
>
> Under the laws in most states, a limited partnership has certain features formerly associated only with corporations. For example, a partnership name may be reserved in advance of formation, and formation is accomplished by filing of its certificate of limited partnership with the designated state office. Limited partners have the right to inspect records and to obtain financial reports similar to those available to corporate shareholders. They also have voting rights and the right to call partnership meetings.
>
> The partnership name normally must end with the words "a limited partnership." If the name of a limited partner appears in the partnership name, it may waive his or her right to limited liability.

This approach can be used to fund specific projects or startup activities. It may even be possible for an existing company to use this approach to fund internal projects. However, *do not try to use this approach without the advice of counsel.*

Consider the case of a large firm with extensive and expensive data processing facilities where a large staff of programmers are busily implementing software needed by the firm. If the software being created has potential value as a product, a limited partnership can be formed to implement that product. Funds are collected from the limited partners, the original firm contracts its programmers to the partnership to get the programming done, and the partnership pays the firm for use of its personnel. *The development project initially becomes a revenue item, rather than an expense item, for the firm.*

The partnership can license the firm to use the product, and the firm will pay the partnership a royalty for the license. The partnership can then arrange for the product to be marketed, and the firm and the partnership will share in any up-front payments and ensuing royalties.

Another Perspective

We administered questionnaires to students in an evening MBA program. Fifty questionnaires were returned. The students worked during the day. The type of jobs held by the respondents were executive management (8%), marketing or sales (28%), and product-related (44%).

Their perspective on the business planning process was that of outsiders looking in. Only a few had ever assisted with a business plan. Our questions to them were not for the purpose of developing expert knowledge; rather, we were interested in their perspectives on what we considered to be several key issues. Some interesting responses were obtained.

Taking a Risk

Only half of the group would invest their own money in a venture. The other half expected someone else to bear the risk. Yet virtually all the successful founders who responded to our questionnaires invested their own money in their ventures.

The Best Way to Get Funded

We asked the respondents to rate the various sources of funding on a scale of 1 to 6, with 1 being the most effective and 6 being the least effective. The average rankings obtained were as follows:

Venture capital	2.89
Sophisticated investors	2.89
Family	3.51
Current employer	3.66

Bank loans	3.76
Other companies	4.11

Venture capital and sophisticated investors were ranked as the best ways to obtain funding, yet our other data showed that these sources reject a high percentage of plans—even if they have solid referrals. Although bank loans were ranked relatively low, many of the successful founders with whom we spoke have bank loans in their portfolios.

What Does It Take to Succeed?

We asked the respondents to give us a list of what they believed to be the key success ingredients for a business plan and the resulting venture. The answers and the number of respondents who selected them were:

Determination, hard work, perseverance	11
A good product idea	8
Creativity, vision	7
Talent and personality of founder	7
Marketing expertise	6
Timing of venture	5
Good business plan and strategy	5
Cash flow, capital, financial management	5
Management team	4
Blind luck	4
Customer orientation, concern	2
Business experience and knowledge	2

Most of the founders we spoke with would agree with the item ranked first. Hard work and perseverance are required to succeed. Having a good product also ranked highly.

But look at the remainder of the list! Customer orientation, customer concern, and business knowledge tied for last place while a management team and blind luck were neck and neck for the next-to-last place. Having a good business plan and good financial management ranked only slightly higher than the management team.

A study of the success factors for ventures is apparently in order for those just starting out.

CASE STUDY: Nor-Cote Chemical Company, Inc.

As you may recall, Nor-Cote was discussed as a "short story" in Chapter 2. Here is some information on how Nor-Cote raised capital through its own employees.

Norman G. Woolcott, Jr., the firm's President, was not happy with the 18 percent interest being charged by banks when he was trying to borrow needed cash. Noting that the banks were paying only 6 percent interest on savings accounts, he formulated an idea of selling his employees stock in the firm and of making loans to them at 9 percent, lower than the banks were charging but greater than they were paying.

He disclosed the firm's plans and financial information to the employees. They were allowed to spend up to 10 percent of their salary on stock purchases. Now, virtually all employees are shareholders, and the firm was able to raise $75,000 through the stock sale. Woolcott says that the stock has risen to ten times its value when the purchases began, and the rate of purchase has slowed down. Nor-Cote no longer needs the cash, but the program continues because of its favorable impact on the company and its customers. "Everyone has a piece of the action," he says. "They take more time and attention with customers' needs."

The loan program also worked well, yielding $45,000 in cash. Interest rates have declined, and this program has ended.

5

Assessing Fundamental Requirements

*I know that I am among civilized men because
they are fighting so savagely.*

Voltaire

The Next Crucial Step

Our purpose in this book is to help you *before* you write a business plan.
By looking carefully at your product, the market, and yourselves, you can
determine whether a business plan should be written at all, and, if written,
for what type of audience. As the next step, then, you or your management
team should apply a benchmark that must be met by the product description, the market description, and your analysis. If the fundamental requirements are met, you can complete the marketing, operations, and financial
portions of the business plan. By performing this analysis after a substantial
amount of information gathering has been done, but before the plan is

written, you can determine whether you have chosen the right audience, thereby increasing the likelihood that your plan will be accepted.

The process, which is given in the 14 tables at the end of this chapter, is not unlike some steps in a due diligence study conducted by a professional investment firm. A due diligence study is conducted for two reasons. First, it can help convince the firm that the opportunity described in a business plan is real and that the plan itself is sound. Second, it can be used by the firm to help prove, during a subsequent lawsuit, that all reasonable steps were taken to determine that the investment was sound.

From our discussions in preparing this book, we learned that firms analyze the business plans they receive in different ways, each using its own screening method. For example, something that may be a top priority to one firm may rank third to another or may be ignored altogether.

The material presented here has some limitations, which should be considered before proceeding.

Some subjectivity remains in the analysis, in spite of our best efforts to define a method based only on objective fact. This shows up in two places:

1. Determining the readability of the product description (Figure 5-1)
2. Evaluating the management team (Figure 5-2)

The first depends on an analysis of how well a layperson understands the material. The second uses a binary scoring scheme to rate an individual's performance. The performance can be rated as either bad or good— that is, either black or white, with no shades of gray. (The field of personnel performance evaluation is beyond the scope of this book, and we chose to use a simple system. You may choose instead to replace the binary scoring system used here with a more sophisticated approach.)

The procedure suggested here has not been used enough to provide a valid numerical profile of how plans ought to look. Although we will provide some suggestions for analysis, each business plan must be analyzed on its own merits.

Our arrangement of factors may differ from that which you prefer. For example, we consider competitive products in the *product* definition whereas others may prefer to include it in the *market* definition. Keep in mind that it is very important to include all factors and that the sequence in which they appear is less important.

Finally, feel free to redesign the forms and procedures to suit your particular use. You should, however, preserve the intent: that is, to provide a rigorous test for marketing and product data and to analyze a management team as objectively as possible.

The Assessment Process

The assessment process outlined in Figures 5-1 through 5-14 can be used to analyze the fundamental requirements and compute a score for market, product, and management team information that will eventually appear in your plan.

Objectivity is the Key

The assessment process should not be regarded as a set of hard and fast rules, although it will be easy to interpret them that way. Instead, think of it as a series of guidelines that we have developed as a result of interviews and discussions with representatives of venture capital firms and SBICs, as well as with founders of firms that have received funding. Since the points itemized in the figures reflect information obtained from many sources, they may appear to be more stringent than any single professional investment firm would require. If that is the case and the guidelines presented do not suit your specific situation, then change them to meet your needs. The key is to keep the assessment process as objective as possible.

Each of the four areas in this analysis is described below—that is, evaluating:

1. Product description
2. Market description
3. Management team
4. Business plan overall

Review the Product Description (Figures 5.1 through 5.7)

Evaluate the product description you have written by considering the following factors and determining a score for each.

Product Description Completeness Score

Check whether the specific items of information in Figure 5.1 have been included in your product description. Score one point for each item included. Explanations for these factors can be found in the first half of Chapter 2.

Figure 5.1 Product description completeness score.

Each of the following is a component of a product description. Enter "1" in the appropriate box if the component is included in the description; enter "O" if it is not included.

1. For a product: What does it do?
   For a service: What does it deliver?

2. Who are the customers?

3. What makes it different?

4. How complex is it?

5. What is the risk of trying it?

6. What are the results of its use?

7. Why would the customer buy it?

8. What is it physically?

9. What training is required?

10. What regulations are relevant?

Total all entries for a Product Description Completeness Score

Product Description Readability Score

Determine the readability of your product description, as suggested in Chapter 2, by asking a layperson to read it. His or her reaction to the description is the basis for the readability score, as shown in Figure 5.2. Your score for this factor can range from 0 to 5.

Complexity of Product Score

Figure 5.3 provides a rating scale for product complexity, ranging from 0 to 5 points. If the categories shown do not apply to your specific situation, they can be revised.

If the product is complex, special training may be required for installing and servicing it. Ongoing maintenance problems can develop in such products. If multiple system components are involved, and training is required for each component, then the complexity increases significantly.

A system component is regarded as a major physical product. In a stereo system, for example, there could be five system components; tuner, amplifier, tape deck, compact disk player, and graphic equalizer. The fact that one amplifier may contain more printed circuit boards than another is not a concern when counting system components.

The meaning of the resulting score (0 to 5) depends on the product. For example, 5 would be the ideal score in a case where the rule is "the simpler the better." A child's toy or a household appliance might fall into this category. In a case where complexity means that maximum function and value are being provided, then 0 is the ideal score. In this instance, you may want to subtract the score on the table from 5 to be consistent with the other measures where higher means better.

Ease of Product Use Score

Highly specialized products may require that customers or users have special skills beyond training in how to use the product—for example, a CAT scanner must be used by a highly trained technician and a medical doctor. The scale in Figure 5.4 ranges from 0 to 5.

The resulting score is neither good nor bad. As with the complexity measure obtained in Figure 5.3, for some products "simpler is better" whereas for others, complexity produces more functionality with a reduction in ease of use. In cases where ease of use is better, 5 would be an

Figure 5.2 Product description readability score.

Each of the following statements evaluates the readability of the product description. Choose the most appropriate scores for each reader (this table considers a sampling of three readers), and place them in the boxes below. Take the average of all the scores and place it in the "Readability Score" box.

It was easily understood by laypersons, with
no explanation.   5

It was understood by laypersons, with clarifications.   4

Laypersons understood enough to ask questions but   3
they could not understand it completely.

Laypersons formed an incorrect impression.   2

Laypersons understood it only with author's explanation.   1

It was not understandable.   0

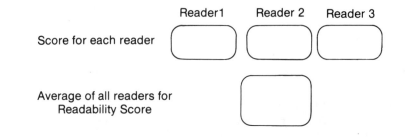

ideal score. In cases where a high skills level and much training are expected, then 0 would be a more appropriate result.

Some samples scores are given as follows:

Product	*Score*
Toaster, garden sprinkler	5
Microwave oven	4
Personal computer system	3 or 2
Mainframe computer system, CAD/CAM Workstation	0

Figure 5.3 Complexity of product score.

Training, installation requirements, the number of major components, and maintenance requirements are evaluated to score the complexity of the product. Choose scores as indicated below, and enter them in the boxes at the right. Add the scores for a total, and compute the final "Complexity Score".

Is more than minimal training needed?   1 = no
                                               0 = yes

Is an installation procedure required?   1 = no
                                               0 = yes

Is ongoing maintenance needed?   1 = no
                                               0 = yes

Enter (number of system components) — 1
See text for definition of *system components*

Total all Scores

Subtract the total from 5 for
the complexity score. If the result   **Complexity Score**
is negative, make it zero.

Results of Product Use Score

A potential marketing problem arises if the results of product use are not visible to the customer, should be quantifiable, and should have demonstrable value. It must be possible to communicate information about the product and its benefits to potential customer. Figure 5.5 offers a method of scoring these factors. Score 1 point for each of the factors that applies to your product.

Figure 5.4 Ease of product use score.

Each of the following statements evaluates the ease with which the product can be used. Select the statement that best describes the ease of use of the product and enter the score at the right of the statement in the"Ease Of Use Score" box.

The product can be used with little or no training.	5
One to five days of in-house training is required.	4
A classroom setting at another location of from one to five days is needed.	3
Special skills and one to five days of training are needed.	2
Special skills and five or more days of training are needed.	1
Special skills and much training are needed.	0

Ease of Use Score

Manufacture or Service Delivery Score

The process by which a product is manufactured or a service delivered will help to determine the size of investment needed. A range of values is presented in Figure 5.6. The factors in the analysis include the number of locations at which the product is manufactured or the service delivery occurs, the number of steps in the process flow used to manufacture the product, an estimate of the kind of capital investment required, whether or not subcontractors are involved, and whether new technology must be developed for production. You choose values from a range of 0 to 5.

Figure 5.5 Results of product use score.

The results of product use are evaluated using such factors as the visibility of results to the user, the degree to which the results can be quantified, and the ease with which the results can be described. Select the appropriate score for each of the factors shown below and place it in the box at the right of each factor. Total all answers and place the result in the "Results of Use Score" box.

Are the results visible?   1 = yes
                                       0 = no

Are the results quantifiable?   1 = yes
                                       0 = no

Are the results valuable?   1 = yes
                                       0 = no

Can the results be described?   1 = yes
                                       0 = no

Are the results understood without   1 = yes
description?   0 = no

Results of Use Score

Product or Service Development Needs Score

The stage of development of a product or service will partly determine both the amount of investment required and the type of investor that may be interested. In Figure 5.7 the various stages in a product life cycle are shown and, on a scale of 0 to 5, you score one point for each stage that has been completed. If audiences other than the professional investment firms are interested in products in early stages of development, you score from 0 to 3. Each of the scores computed is judged independently because the worth, or importance, of specific scores depends on the product.

Figure 5.6 Manufacture/service delivery score.

Manufacture or service delivery is evaluated using such factors as the number of locations involved, whether one or several processes are involved, the amount of capital investment needed, whether sub-contractors are used, and whether the technology needed for production is available. Select the appropriate score for each of the factors shown below and place it in the box to the right of each factor. Total all answers and place the result in the "Manufacture or Service Delivery Score" box.

Is only one location used?

1 = yes
0 = no

Is one manufacturing process used?

1 = yes
0 = no

Is a low or high capital investment required?

1 = low
0 = high

Are subcontractors involved?

1 = yes
0 = no

Is the technology available?

1 = yes
0 = no

Manufacture or Service Delivery Score

Review the Market Description
(Figures 5.8 to 5.11)

Evaluate the market description material that you have gathered by considering the following factors and determining a score for each.

Figure 5.7 Product/service development needs score.

The stage of development for the product score is based on the product life cycle stages that the product has been through. For each of the factors below, score "1" if the factor has been done. "0" if it has not been done. Place the score in the box at the right of the factor. Add all factors to produce the "Product/Service Development Needs Score."

Concept formulation complete

Concept tested

General design completed

Detail design completed

Prototype completed

Limited production completed

Full production in process

Product/Service Development Needs Score

Market Description Completeness Score

Check whether the specific items of information in Figure 5.8 have been considered in your market description. Score one point for each item included. Explanations for these factors can be found in the second half of Chapter 2.

Figure 5.8 Market description completeness score.

Each of the following is a component of a market description. Enter "1" in the appropriate box if the component is included in the description, "O" if it is not.

Who are the customers?

How do you know they want the product?

How did you set the price?

How did you determine the market share?

What prevents you from achieving your goals?

Where are the customers?

How can you market the product to your customers?

How can you get the product to your customers?

What customer service is required?

What training is required?

Market Description Completeness Score

Figure 5.9 Market potential score.

The market potential is scored after the market size and product price have been determined. The estimated annual revenue after five years of operation is used to determine the score. Find the appropriate factor below and enter the value shown in the "Market Potential Score" box.

$100M or greater	5
$50M-$100M	4
$20M-$50M	3
$10M-$20M	2
$5M-$10M	1
Less than $5M	0

Market Potential Score ⬚

Market Potential Score

The market potential is determined after market size and price have been estimated. (See Figure 5.9) The amount of estimated annual revenues after five years will greatly affect the kind of investor that you may be able to attract. With annual revenues of $50 million or greater, almost any investment group would be interested. Revenues in the $20 to $50 million range will still interest many firms though because that level of revenue would support a public stock offering. For plans that show revenues in the $10 million category and under, it may be easier to form a strategic alliance with an interested corporate partner than to get professional investment funds. Figure 5.9 illustrates ranges of revenues and assigns a score to each.

Market Awareness Score

The factors and values assigned to market awareness are presented in Figure 5.10. The degree to which the market is aware of the need for your type of product, similar products, and your specific product will help determine the degree of difficulty and expense involved in a marketing program.

Figure 5.10 Market awareness score.

The ease of communicating the nature of this product to its market is estimated using such factors as awareness of need, awareness of product type, awareness of this *specific* product, the number of competitors, and the dominance of the market leader. Select the appropriate answer for each factor and enter it in the box to the right. Total all answers for the "Market Awareness Score."

General awareness of need	1= yes 0= no	
General awareness of this product type	1= yes 0= no	
General awareness of this *particular* product	1= yes 0= no	
More than two competitors	0= yes 1= no	
One competitor dominant	0= yes 1= no	
Market Awareness Score		

Sources of Market Information Score

Many of the different sources of information that can be used to estimate market size are covered in Figure 5.11. You earn one point for each source that has been used in preparation of your market information.

The Founders or the Management Team

This is one of the first areas in a business plan to receive close attention from any professional investment firm. In the method presented here, the

Figure 5.11 Market information score.

There are many sources of market information. The number of sources that were used in preparing the market description is scored. For each of the sources listed below, score a "1" if the source was used and backup data are available, and score "O" if they are not. Total all answers for the "Market Information Score."

Customer surveys

Market rocoaroh   Outside

Market research—Inside

Trade association data

Focus groups

Suppliers / Distributors

Trade literature

Published market data

Inquiries by prospects

Pre-sales

Orders

Market Information Score

skills needed in your business venture are determined first. The criteria for judging those skills are then developed and a "Total Ideal Score" is computed. Skills and experience in the available founders or management team are then assessed, and a "Total Available Score" is computed. Finally, a "Grade" is determined by dividing the Total Available Score by the Total Ideal Score.

This method will force the founders or management team to see themselves as an outsider might see them. Missing skills can easily be spotted and action taken to correct deficiencies.

Founder/Management Team Functional Skills

In Chapter 3, a Skills Matrix was developed (Figure 3.1). If you have developed this matrix for your business venture, you have already created a list of the functional skills required. In Figure 5.12, the available functional skills are evaluated for the founders or the management team. It provides a form on which you may list the functions performed by each individual on your management team and then compute an overall grade for the team.

The grade for each function is based on the number of years each individual has had experience at the function, the projects he or she has initiated, the projects which were successful, overall performance, and job-related education. You score one point for each factor that applies to a function. The maximum possible score for an individual is equal to five times the number of functions listed.

The factors of "Initiated Projects" and "Successful Projects" are meant to be indicators of an individual's ability to identify what needs to be done and to do it successfully. High-scorers are the kind of people who should be a part of your business venture. Give the "Performance Good" factor a 1 or 0 value for simplicity. (It is possible to use a 1 to 5 rating system, for example, by changing the computations as necessary on Figures 5.13 and 5.14.)

When the individual's name and functions have been entered in the table (1), the factors are then scored (2). Each row of factors is added to produce a subtotal (3), and the subtotals are added to produce the individual total (4).

Use one copy of this table for each person on the team.

Grade the Team

Figure 5.13 enables you to compute a team grade. The individual names and number of functions listed in Figure 5.12 are entered on the form in Figure 5.13. The "Ideal Score" is computed by multiplying the

Figure 5.12 Evaluation of management team functional skills.

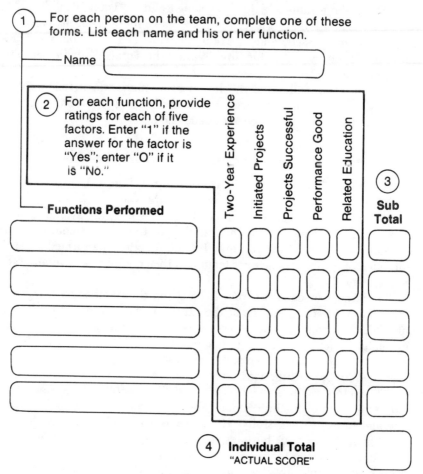

number of functions for each individual by 5. The "Actual Score" is transcribed from Figure 5.12 and entered here. The grade is then computed by dividing the "Actual Score" (B) by the "Ideal Score" (A).

All "Ideal Scores" are added to produce a *team* "Ideal Score." All "Actual Scores" are similarly summed. A "Team Grade" is computed by dividing the "Team Actual Total" (D) by the "Team Ideal Score" (C).

If any of the founders has financial, legal, or tax problems, they could become a greater problem if he or she assumes equity in a new venture. Note any such problems as part of this process on a set of notes, as there is no place in the tables for this kind of information.

Figure 5.13 Management team grade.

The results of the Functional Skills Evaluation (Figure 5.12) are determined by comparing actual scores with "ideal" scores. A percentage grade is computed for each individual and for the management team as a whole.

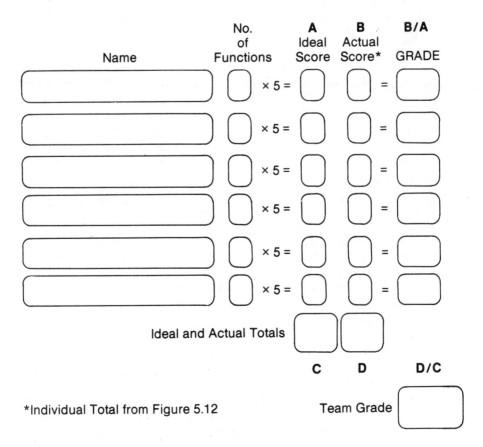

*Individual Total from Figure 5.12

Business Plan Analysis Summary

The criteria outlined in this chapter are useful in forcing an objective look at the basics behind your business plan. You may benefit greatly by doing the analyses suggested. Once completed, you will have to study the scores carefully in order to understand their message.

   Figure 5.14 provides a convenient way to summarize the individual scores obtained and to compare them with the "ideal" values. Comments on each of the factors follow:

Product Description Completeness Score   The score here should be as high as possible. Ideally, all eleven components of the product description have been entered in the form in Figure 5.1.

Product Description Readability Score   Scores of 4 or 5 are acceptable. Lower scores in Figure 5.2 indicate either that a major rewrite is necessary or that the product cannot be easily described or understood by the layperson. If this is the case, then your product is probably of interest only to technical specialists in your field.

Complexity of Product Score   There is no right or wrong score in Figure 5.3. Obviously, a product like a large computer system is intended to be complex, while a product like the hula hoop is meant to be simple. The complexity should be appropriate to the customer and to the amount and skill level of maintenance planned for the product.

Ease of Product Use Score   Again, there is no right or wrong answer in Figure 5.4. In general, the easier the product is to use, the better for any customer.

Results of Product Use Score   The higher the score in Figure 5.5, the better. Results that are quantifiable and visible are very desirable for use in marketing literature.

Manufacture/Service Delivery Score   In general, the higher the score in Figure 5.6, the better. Intentionally complex products may be unavoidably complex to manufacture; however, even for these products, it is wise to simplify the process as much as possible. Every unnecessary complexity costs money and increases the likelihood of errors, breakdowns, and failures.

Product/Service Development Needs Score   Again, the higher the score in Figure 5.7, the better. The more completely developed your product or service is, the easier it will be to approach professional investors for help.

Market Description Completeness Score   A score of 10 is ideal in Figure 5.8 because that means you have included all components of the market description in your business plan.

Market Potential Score   High scores in Figure 5.9 mean high revenues for your company.

Market Awareness Score   A high score in Figure 5.10 means that the job of marketing will be simplified, thereby reducing the expense and improving your chances for success.

Sources of Market Information Score   The maximum score of 11 is best in Figure 5.11, but it is unlikely that you will be able to get information from all eleven sources listed. Again, the higher the score, the better.

Functional Skills Analysis Score   The highest score possible in Figure

Figure 5.14 Business plan analysis summary.

The scores from Figures 5.1-5.13 are recorded here in order to compute a grade for each part of the analysis. The actual scores are divided by the highest possible score for each factor to produce a decimal fraction between 0 and 1. You may total all Grades and divide by 12 to produce an Overall Plan Grade.

	Actual Score	Ideal Score	Grade
Product Description Completeness Score	☐	/10=	☐
Product Description Readability Score	☐	/5=	☐
Complexity of Product Score	☐	/5=	☐
Ease of Product Use Score	☐	/5=	☐
Results of Product Use Score	☐	/5=	☐
Manufacture/Service Delivery Score	☐	/5=	☐
Product/Service Development Needs Score	☐	/7=	☐
Market Description Completeness Score	☐	/10=	☐
Market Potential Score	☐	/5=	☐
Market Awareness Score	☐	/5=	☐
Sources of Market Information Score	☐	/11=	☐
Functional Skills Analysis Score / Management Team Grade Score	☐	/1=	☐

5.12 is five times the number of functions listed. That is also the "ideal" score.

Management Team Grade Score   A score of 100% is best in Figure 5.13, but a founding team would rarely attain it. The grade at which a go or no-go decision is made is subjective, but specific missing skills in marketing or finance, or missing leadership skills, should be warning signs. If only product development skills are available, then you should acquire additional management talent or deal with a corporate partner who has an interest in your product line. You may also work with a professional investor who will build your management team for you. In rare cases, you may discover that a VC firm will overlook all shortcomings and help build your venture. Don't count on it.

When you have assessed the results obtained from analyses of the factors listed in Figure 5.14, make your decision as to whether to proceed. If you decide against it, you should have very specific information from this analysis to tell you what additional work needs to be done.

6

The Components of a Business Plan

As you know, there are many possible audiences for your business plan, and the choice of audience depends on what you want it to accomplish. In this chapter, we will concentrate on the type of business plan you might send to a venture capital firm. In Chapter 7, we will discuss modifying the standard outline to meet the needs of other audiences it might appeal to.

Through our interviews and questionnaires, we found that a business plan is usually originated by people with a product or service idea—especially to technical people involved with the product and its delivery. Marketing and financial people are often not available at the start of a business venture, and these are the skills most often missing in a new venture. Based on our findings, we have made some key assumptions.

Readers of this book will most probably:

- Be on the product or technical side of a venture
- Not have a financial or marketing person available to help with a plan
- Will not have the money to hire either an accountant or a market research firm to help develop the initial plan

Therefore, on these pages we stress marketing and financial topics. Introductory marketing information may be found in Chapter 2. Basic financial information may be found in this chapter.

In our interviews, company founders told us that effective controls on the expenses and operation of the firm as well as clear and concise reporting of production and financial matters were important to their success. Investors with whom we spoke also agreed that these issues were very important; when ventures they had funded were in trouble, controls and reporting were often the first things that had to be implemented to turn them around. Yet, in the questionnaires returned to us, few responses indicated that any control and reporting issues had been included in the business plans. Further, in the business plan outlines we obtained, these topics were frequently not mentioned at all.

If controls and reporting are implemented to save a company, why not implement them from the beginning to help keep the company out of trouble? We suggest including such controls in the business plan, and implementing them from the beginning in the business venture. This information will let everyone interested in a venture know whether it is on or off plan, and provide early warning if something is going wrong.

The Business Plan Outline

There is no perfect sequence for the contents of a business plan. Each reader may want to see sections in a different order or to see different information emphasized. We suggest the following outline, developed as a result of our interviews with professional investors—many of whom mentioned specific groups of information that should be included and the sequence in which they look for them. The investors also mentioned "funding by milestones," as did several of the company founders we interviewed.

The length of the business plan will depend on your product, its stage of development, and the amount of money you are seeking. If you are involved in a startup with a product that requires little development and you want only $50,000 to $100,000 in seed capital, your plan will be short—perhaps only 15 to 20 pages. However, if you are starting a major venture requiring heavy capital investment in manufacturing facilities for a nationwide consumer product, the business plan and the research and supporting data could be a hundred pages or more. The basic outline is presented below.

Table of Contents

The reader must be able to find all topics in the text and all illustrations or tables you have included. The length of the table of contents will depend on the number of topics and illustrations to be listed. (A sample from the EXUS business plan appears later in this chapter.)

Executive Summary

The executive summary, a concise summary of the business plan, is critical to its success. You must be able to describe the product and its market opportunity in summary form if you want the remainder of the plan to be reviewed. The summary should include:

- A brief background on the founders
- A short description of the product
- A short market description
- Key financial data, including the amount of money you need and how it will be used

The information included here will serve to interest the reader in the rest of the plan. The executive summary should be two or three pages in length. (A sample from the EXUS business plan is included in this chapter.)

The Management Team

Who are the people involved with the product and the business plan? What role will each individual play if the plan is funded? What skills are missing from the group of people involved, which are necessary to make the product a success?

Background information for each of the participants, including positions held and key accomplishments, should be given in brief narrative style. The educational accomplishments of each participant should be mentioned also. Other information, such as age and other personal information, will help the reader get to know the management team. The length of this section will depend on the number of people involved, their backgrounds, and their accomplishments.

The Product

What is the product? What does it do? What are its physical attributes? What is its present stage of development? What makes it unique? This section should clearly describe the product and make it real for the readers of the plan. If available, drawings or photographs should be included.

The Market for the Product

Who are the potential customers for the product? Why would they buy it? Do they alone make the decision to buy or do they need to get approval from others? Are the customer and user the same individual? What would a potential customer pay for the product? What competition exists? How does this product differ from the competition? How do you plan to exploit the difference? Include numerical information that describes the market, using graphic presentations as much as possible.

Marketing Plan

How can potential customers be contacted, and how can those contacts be converted to sales? How will the competition respond? What can be done to deal with responses from competitors? How much market penetration will be achieved, and when? Prepare projections for "Sales (Unit) Volume and Returns."

Operational Plan

How do the founders intend to use the funding obtained? How do they intend to run the company, if one is formed? How do they intend to market, build, and distribute the product? This portion of the plan should tie together the product, marketing, and financial sections of the business plan into a unified approach toward running the venture.

Financial Analysis

What will the marketing and operational plans cost? What are the revenue projections? How much money do you have? How much money do you need? If investors choose to fund the business plan, when and how can they expect a return, and in what form? At least these computations should be included:

Sales forecast and pro forma income statement
Cash flow analysis
Pro forma balance sheet
Source and use of funds

Optionally, key ratios might show the following:

Return on equity
Current ratio
Working capital
Debt-to-equity
Net worth

These are explained following this outline.

Objectives and Milestones

What objectives and milestones will be used to measure progress in marketing, operations, and finance? What measures will tell both company founders and investors that everything is on track or that something needs attention? The length of this portion of the business plan could be two or three pages. (Examples are presented later in this chapter.)

Controls and Reporting

What controls and reports will allow company founders and investors know that the plan is being successfully executed, that milestones are being met, and that funds are being spent properly? One or two pages will suffice here. Additional discussion is found below.

Ownership and Equity

How will equity in the venture be distributed? Will the founders retain control? Will employees be able to earn equity for their performance? How much equity will funders have, and how will that change over time? How do the investors get their money out, and when?

Appendices

Appendices contain data that is too detailed to include in the body of the plan but is necessary to its analysis. Data included here may also serve to show that you have done your homework in preparing the plan.

The amount of information in the appendices depends on the amount of detail needed to back up your plan; for short plans, appendices may not be needed at all.

When professional investors develop an interest in a business plan, they will ask their technical specialists to examine it. If the appendices are prepared as separate documents and are hand-delivered directly to each specialist, you will protect the confidentiality of your material by ensuring that each person is given only the detail he or she needs to answer specific questions. The following topics are likely to be found in appendices:

- Product specifications—Including designs, tests, prototype information
- Market research results—Including information from any of the sources mentioned in Chapter 2
- Detailed market planning information—Including names of major customers, specifics of the marketing strategy, planned advertising approaches, sales incentives, and compensation
- Detailed financial analyses that serve as backup to the summary information placed in the body of the plan
- Job descriptions, responsibilities, and tasks for key members of the team—especially if recruiting and team organization are included as part of the business plan

On Confidentiality

Separating your business plan materials into a main plan with confidential appendices requires some extra work. However, we believe that this additional effort is useful. Preserving the confidentiality of your material is extremely important because, after all, you have worked hard to develop something of value and others may want to get their hands on the results of your labor.

Many company founders assume that professional investment firms are completely ethical and above reproach and can be expected to treat all your materials as confidential. When we raised the issue of confidentiality and nondisclosure agreements, however, one principal in a venture capital firm angrily told us, "We sign no nondisclosure agreements. We don't have to. The first time we breach a confidence, the word gets out on the street and the business plans stop coming in. We are finished."

We do not want to impugn the integrity of any firm, but we suggest that you carefully read the case study of Precision Image Corporation at the end of this chapter. Here, the principals in a large, well-known venture capital firm had received a presentation from a startup firm looking for first-round funding. The principals had recently funded a direct competitor, which was mentioned as such in the startup's business plan.

Now read the short story entitled "Item on the TV Evening News," also at the end of this chapter. In this case, a founder who was earnestly seeking money from a number of sources became an object of derisive humor on a local TV news program.

Although the vast majority of people involved in the professional investment process are ethical and live up to their responsibility to keep business plan information confidential, even one exception can do you great harm. Therefore, we recommend that you take great care to ensure that the material in your business plan remains confidential. One way to ensure this confidentiality is to have an organized business plan with detailed information on your potential customers, market, product, and finances placed in separate appendices. Other measures will be discussed in Chapter 7.

Pricing

There are many ways to price a product. In your market research, you should strive to identify the pricing method used by your competition. If you are marking up cost plus 10 percent and the competition is marking it up 5 to 1, you will miss a revenue opportunity; if the situation is reversed, you will lose sales. Choose the most appropriate method and include a description and rationale for it in the marketing section of your plan.

The Executive Summary

This is the most important part of any business plan. Principals in the venture capital firms we interviewed agree that a business plan must quickly convince them that it deserves to be read in detail. "I can size up a business plan in about three minutes," one principal told us. "First, I look at the summary. Then I look at the management team. Then, the financials. I look for readability, completeness, and credibility. If it doesn't pass the test, I don't finish reading it." Since this is the first part of your business plan that most readers will see, the executive summary must be especially well written.

The executive summary should describe the major elements of the business plan such as the product and its unique aspects, the market, the management team, the investment needed, and the financial opportunity. It should also briefly describe the business plan itself, summarizing the various materials that have been included therein. You should mention here that you also have several detailed appendices that are confidential and will be provided at the appropriate time.

Financial Analysis

The financial portion of the business plan discusses time frames and computations. The construction of these analyses is important, but the accounting and financial reporting discipline may be new to you. As when using another language to communicate—such as French, engineering jargon, or computerese—you have to know the terminology and vocabulary. If you follow generally accepted rules when preparing the reports, they will be more easily understood by your audience, thereby enhancing your credibility.

You may not need an accountant to prepare an initial set of reports. The information in this chapter along with other sources of information should help you with a first set of financial information in a startup situation. If your plan is complicated, or if you have trouble with the data, you may want to seek help from an accountant. As you deal with professional investors on a major venture, you will be probably be asked to engage a recognized public accounting firm.

Every existing company or startup will have its own set of expense and revenue items, as well as its own time frame considerations, for its business plan. Therefore, every set of financial reports will be unique. The EXUS business plan, which is serving as our sample throughout this book, differs slightly from the idealized set of descriptions we will provide below. However, the guidelines we give you will provide a useful starting point, and you may add your own variations as needed.

There are several popular personal computerized spread sheets available on preprogrammed software, which accept basic revenue and expense data and are supposed to produce "all the reports you need for a business plan." If you use one of these packages, make sure you can explain each of the reports you are using. Including these standardized reports in your business plan implies that you have accounting and financial skills. If you cannot explain them or effectively answer questions, it will damage your credibility.

On the following pages we will discuss the format of each report or analysis and explain how each one is prepared. Note that specific accounting rules apply to the items included on each report, which we do not discuss. For example, we have not attempted to give you guidance in your choice of depreciation methods or computation of tax liabilities because these topics are beyond the scope of this book. In the bibliography, however, we list several reference books that can help in these areas. You can also engage an accountant to help.

Time Frame and Level of Detail

We asked partners in three of the Big Eight accounting firms for advice on how far into the future, and at what level of detail, a business plan should project. All of these experts agreed that the business plan should cover between three and five years of future operation. For a business currently in operation, they suggest adding two to three years worth of past financial reports to support the data on the current operating year. When asked about the level of detail to be shown in each year of the plan, however, each firm gave us a different answer:

Firm 1: First-year projections should be shown on a monthly basis; the second-year projections on a quarterly basis, and third- through fifth-year projections, annually.

Firm 2: The first- and second-year projections should be shown on a quarterly basis, with annual projections thereafter.

Firm 3: The first two years should show monthly projections, with quarterly projections thereafter.

The EXUS Company business plan uses quarterly projections for the first 18 months and annual data thereafter.

We suggest that you choose whatever level of detail best allows readers of your business plan to see the critical future events in the life of your business venture. If a quarterly level of detail obscures critical monthly events, then consider providing monthly detail. The financial data should be of sufficient detail to allow the reader to find all the major milestones mentioned in the business plan.

Whatever information you include, be prepared to provide more in response to questions from readers of your business plan because they will want to know how you developed these reports.

Sales (Unit) Volume and Returns

Project the number of units to be sold in each of the time intervals included in the plan. When projecting sales volumes, allow sufficient time in your forecast for product development and marketing activities. Estimate how many units you expect to be returned, and subtract this from units sold to produce net unit volume. Use data describing your competitors' business to estimate volume of returns.

If your plan is to improve quality within an existing company, then make appropriate reductions in the projections. If you have no comparable data to use, use various statistical quality control techniques that purport to predict product failure.

Sales Forecast and Pro Forma Income Statement

Before preparing this report, determine the price you will charge for your product and how that price will vary over the life of the plan. If, for example, you are manufacturing a consumer electronics item, you might expect the price to start high and decrease as the competition heats up because this is the pattern shown with other products in the computer industry.

The items included in this report are as follows:

Net Sales　Multiply the unit price for each time period by the net unit volume to be sold for that period. Adjust the revenue for each period to account for collections. For example, you may assume that 20 percent of sales are in cash, that 60 percent will be paid within 30 days, that 18 percent will be paid in 60 days, and that 2 percent is uncollectible. Document your assumptions.

Cost of Sales　For each time interval, determine the cost of materials and labor involved in making the product, as well as the overhead costs that apply to your product. Add these amounts to produce your *cost of sales*. Compute material costs using detailed bills of materials, and obtain price quotes. Compute labor costs using time standards for manufacture, and document the times and salary information used.

Gross Margin　For each time interval, compute sales less cost of sales to show your *gross margin*.

Operating Expense　For each time interval, determine the amount of money to be spent on R&D on the product. Then compute the general and administrative (C&A) expenses to be encountered. Add all these figures to produce your *operating expense*. Document planned R&D activities, using your marketing plan as a backup for your marketing expense, and document all the expenses included in the G&A category.

Operating Profit (Loss)   For each time interval, compute your company's gross margin less operating expenses to show your *operating profit or loss*.

Misc. Income   Identify all nonsales sources of *miscellaneous income* such as interest earned, product consulting fees, and so on. Document each item included.

Net Income (Loss) Before Taxes   For each time interval, compute operating profit (loss) plus misc. income to show your *net pretax income or loss*.

Taxes on Income   Document any taxes owing on *net income before taxes*.

Net Income (Loss)   For each interval, compute: net income before taxes less taxes on income to show your net income or loss.

Explain any seasonal variations you anticipate (frequently found in retail sales), and discuss price or volume discounts if they affect your sales projections.

Explain and document every assumption you make in preparing the numbers used in your projections. It is popular to use an assumption of 20 percent annual growth in sales, for example. If you make this assumption, explain why you think that it is reasonable. If the published actual growth rate of competitive firms in your industry is 20 percent and the market in general has a documented annual growth rate of 20 percent, then your numbers are probably good.

It is suggested that you do not use another popular assumption for determining cost of goods sold. This assumption is that cost of goods sold is 50 percent of the sales price. Although it may apply in some cases, it does not apply in others. Whatever percentage you do show, be prepared for many questions on the material, labor, and overhead expenses that went into determining it.

You can also compute similar *operating ratios* for every item in your sales forecast and pro forma income statement. If your ratios are appreciably different from those of similar firms, then be prepared to explain why.

Cash Flow Analysis

A cash flow analysis should be prepared and should cover the same time periods selected for the sales forecast and pro forma income statement.

The items to include in your cash flow analysis are described below.

Beginning Cash Balance　Available cash at the start of the period.

Cash Receipts　Total cash received during the period from sources identified on the sales forecast and pro forma income statement.

Cash Disbursements　Expenses for accounts payable, miscellaneous expenses, and all tax payments.

Net Cash From Operations　For each time interval, compute your beginning cash balance plus cash receipts less cash disbursements to show your net cash from operations.

Sale of Stock　Cash received from the sale of stock.

Purchase of Assets　Cash spent for anything that becomes an asset of the firm such as equipment, computers, computer software, and buildings.

Funds Invested　An increase or decrease in the amount of cash invested. If you and your co-founders plan to put your own money into the venture, it should be reflected here.

Short-Term Debt　Cash used to repay short-term debt.

Long-Term Debt　Cash used to repay long-term debt.

Ending Cash Balance　For each time interval, compute net cash from operations plus cash from sale of stock less cash for purchase of assets plus cash invested (less cash removed) less cash used to repay debt.

If you have not already done so in the pro forma income statement, you may want to state here, in the cash flow analysis, any assumptions concerning receivables for a particular time period. You also may want to explain your company's credit policies for customers.

The cash flow analysis is useful for estimating the amount of funding you will need. If you do not include funds invested or stock sale revenues, the ending cash balance will probably go negative rather quickly. As revenues increase, however, the ending cash balance will increase and eventually go positive. The largest negative number is, in theory, the amount of funding you will need. Prudent managers and investors will add a contingency amount to the ending cash balance in order to provide for various kinds of surprises.

The timing of funds to be received will depend on two factors:

1. Your research, marketing, and operational plans, which will describe the activities that require funds and the times at which they are needed.
2. The investors will probably control the rate at which you receive funds. They may use objectives and milestones in the business plan to determine when funds should be made available. The cash flow analysis may be prepared again by a professional investor but, as you write the plan, you should have concrete ideas about what you want to do, when you want to do it, and how much it will cost. This information will allow you to complete your cash flow analysis.

When funding increments and timing have been determined, you should be able to enter the appropriate amounts in the cash flow analysis. The ending cash balance should always be equal to or greater than the contingency amount that you have established for your business venture or firm.

Pro Forma Balance Sheet

A pro forma balance sheet should be prepared for each year projected in your business plan. This will reflect in aggregate many of the decisions you have made on asset management and capital investments. Any assumptions you have made should be clearly stated.

The items included in this report are presented below.

Assets include all cash or goods that you can use to house and run your company and pay for your liabilities.

Current assets include cash or items that can be converted into cash in a short time—for example, cash, investments, accounts receivable, and inventory. The actual current values for each of these items are added together to produce *total current assets*.

Fixed assets include those items that cannot easily be converted into cash—for example, buildings, property, plant and equipment. Use the depreciated value of these items. These values are added together to produce *total fixed assets*.

Your total current assets and total fixed assets are added together to produce your *total assets*.

Liabilities and Stockholders' Equity

These represent amounts you owe to someone and the equity owed to the stockholders.

Current liabilities include accounts payable, taxes payable, and short-term debt—that is, any amount that has to be paid in the short term. These values are added together to produce *current liabilities*.

Long-term debt includes items that have to be repaid over a long period of time. These values are added together to produce *total long-term debt*.

Stockholders' equity includes outstanding stock in the firm and retained earnings. Current values for preferred stock, common stock, and retained earnings are added together to produce *total equity*.

Your *current liabilities, total long-term debt,* and *stockholders' equity* are added together to produce *total liabilities and stockholders' equity*.

Key Financial Ratios or Measures

Key financial ratios or measures can be computed from information in the analyses described on the preceding pages to help in analyzing your business plan. Readers of your plan will check these ratios to see whether they are reasonable and how they compare with those of similar firms. Several important ratios or measures are described below.

Return on equity is computed by dividing net income (from the income statement) by total equity (from the balance sheet). Where multiple values are encountered, an annual average is used.

Current ratio is computed by dividing current assets by current liabilities. Both values are on the balance sheet.

Working capital is computed by subtracting current liabilities from current assets. (Both values are on the balance sheet.)

Debt to equity is computed by dividing total liabilities by total equity.

Net worth is the total equity, and it shows your ability to sustain losses as they occur.

Sources and Uses of Funds

The source and use report is not recommended in the business plan guidelines published by the Big 8 accounting firms we interviewed, but it is included in some of the effective business plans we have recently looked at. We suggest that you consider including it in the financial analysis section of your business plan.

A source and use report describes every source of funding for a firm and the uses of funds from those sources. It describes what changes in assets are being made and their resulting impact on cash on hand or liabilities of the firm. Such information is of great interest to investors.

To construct this report, calculate the changes in balance sheet items from one year to the next. The change amount is categorized as either a source or use. A *source of funds* is a decrease in an asset item and/or an increase in a liability item. A *use of funds* is an increase in an asset and/ or a decrease in a liability item. (An example of a source and use report appears in the EXUS business plan later in this chapter.)

Objectives and Milestones

Objectives and milestones are specific events in the life of your venture by which you and your investors can measure your performance against the business plan. Some examples of these are:

Hiring of a full management team
Completing product specifications
Completing product design
Completing prototype
First customer shipment
First full quarter of profitability
Attaining $10 million in revenue

You get the idea, don't you?

Controls and Reporting

Once you have established some objectives and milestones you are ready to plan for a series of future reports in two major areas:

1. Overall performance of your firm *against* the objectives and milestones you have set
2. Variations in expenses, project deadlines, production schedules, or other internal occurrences that can cause you to miss your objectives or milestones

This series of reports should include detailed budget and variance analyses as well as the spectrum of customary financial reports. They should be prepared at weekly, monthly, or quarterly intervals, as required.

For objective and milestone reporting, you should first break down each objective and milestone into the tasks that must be performed to reach it. Then you should report on the time and money expended on each task, and the expected or actual date each task will be achieved.

These reports should be used in a regular system of control for the business venture. Individuals should be assigned responsibilities to prepare, read, and act on each report. While routine financial reporting may proceed on a monthly basis, internal operations reports may need to be created weekly, or even daily, if there are problems to be solved. This system of reports should be combined with regularly scheduled board meetings at which financial and operational issues are discussed as appropriate.

Burak also feels strongly about controls. "Controls are absolutely critical," he says. "Without controls, you're just spending money without the slightest idea of where you are.

"Time and cost milestones are a good minimum set for controls. By establishing time milestones, such as:

Product design complete—3 months
Prototype complete—6 months
Testing complete—9 months
Begin production—12 months

"You can clearly define what is completed and what is not. By mapping actual cost to achieve each milestone against the planned cost, you can re-evaluate your position and predict cash shortfalls in time to take action."

By defining these reports as part of your business plan, you are serving notice that you intend to track closely performance against the business plan. This will offer some comfort to potential investors and may prevent the plan from remaining in a desk drawer once it has served its initial purpose.

Ownership and Equity

As we have already discussed, there are several ways to obtain assistance for your firm or business venture. It is possible to:

Use your own money
Take out a loan
Sell equity
Contract for direct help such as using laboratory equipment or computers, or helping with marketing or other special services

A major difference among all these types of assistance is the amount of equity you can or must give up.

The founders we spoke to recommend nonequity funding such as bank loans or deals with other firms. It is only when those sources are inadequate that you should consider selling a piece of your equity.

Valuing Your Business or Your Business Plan

If you choose to deal with a professional investment firm, either you or they will have to determine the dollar value of your company or venture. The amount of money injected into your new venture will, in effect, determine its value. Investors will not want to invest more than it is worth, and determining that worth is not always easy. You and the investors are gambling that your business plan is accurate and that you will achieve the revenues and profits you claim.

The amount of money provided by investors, their expected return on the investment, and the value of the business will determine the amount of equity the investors will ask for.

We found the following concise description of valuation process in a publication of the Big 8 accounting firm of Deloitte, Haskins & Sells, *Raising Venture Capital: An Entrepreneur's Guidebook*, pages 55–56.

Suppose that Omnipresent Synergy, Inc., a start-up company, projects that by its fifth year it will earn $1,000,000 after taxes on sales of $10,000,000. Suppose further that the initial funding request is $800,000 and that the venture capital investors require a 50% compound rate of return on their investment. (NOTE: This assumes that the investors believe the projections are realistic. Because business plans are typically very aggressive and optimistic, they will often make a "risk

adjustment" to your financial analysis by reducing your projected after-tax earnings. The adjusted figure is their basis for
calculating return on investment.)

One method used to determine how the equity should be
split is as follows:

1. The investors will estimate the value of your company
   in the fifth year based on a multiple of earnings for companies similar to yours. Assume that based on the investors' research of your industry, companies similar to
   Omnipresent Synergy, Inc. are selling for approximately
   15 times current earnings. This would give your company a total valuation in year 5 of $15,000,000 (15 ×
   $1,000,000 of earnings).

2. Using this multiple and the required 50% rate of return, you can calculate the present value of the company using the following formula:

$$\text{Present value} = \frac{\text{future valuation}}{(1+i)^n}$$

Where future valuation = total estimated value of
company in 5 years
i = required rate of return
n = number of years

The present value of Omnipresent Synergy, Inc. would be
calculated as follows:[1]

$$\frac{\text{Future valuation}}{(1+i)^n} = \frac{\$15,000,000}{(1+.50)^5} = \frac{\$15,000,000}{7.6} = \$1,975,000$$

[1] This tabulation of present value factors can be used in calculating the pricing structure:

PRESENT VALUE FACTORS

Years	Required rate of return			
	30%	40%	50%	60%
1	1.3	1.4	1.5	1.6
2	1.7	2.0	2.3	2.6
3	2.2	2.7	3.4	4.1
4	2.9	3.8	5.1	6.6
5	3.7	5.4	7.6	10.5
6	4.8	7.5	11.4	16.8
7	6.3	10.5	17.1	26.8

3. Based on the initial required funding of $800,000, the investors' share of the company would be 41%, which is calculated as follows:

$$\frac{\text{Initial funding}}{\text{Present value}} = \frac{\$800,000}{\$1,975,000} = 41\%$$

The table below shows the difference in the investors' share, if the earnings multiples and required rates of return over a five-year period were varied for Omnipresent Synergy, Inc.

INVESTORS' REQUIRED % OWNERSHIP

Earnings multiple	Required rate of return			
	30%	40%	50%	60%
10×	30	43	61	84
15×	20	29	41	56
20×	15	22	30	42
25×	12	17	24	34

The examples and formulas used above may not be used by all venture capitalists, and only apply, of course, to straight-equity investments. They are provided here only as a guide to helping you evaluate what your company is worth to potential investors.

Make Sure You Get What You Need and Want

As you can see by glancing at the "Investors' Required % Ownership" table in the foregoing reprinted publication material, you may have to give up a significant portion of your equity if professional investors get involved. The values in the table range from 12 to 84 percent, but the most likely values are between 40 and 60 percent.

Giving up that much equity may be either positive or negative, depending on your point of view and the ultimate success of the venture. Consider the following example:

The two founders of an electronic assembly company wanted to expand their business. The firm had annual revenues of $800,000 and the salaries of the founders were $50,000 each. Their plan was to go beyond assembling printed circuit boards for other firms and to extend the business into producing their own cards for the personal computer market.

They developed a design for this and sought the necessary funding but were unable to borrow funds. They determined that the only way to get more value from their company was to sell it, but they soon discovered that there were no available buyers. They were, in effect, stuck with the company, each holding 50 percent equity in it.

Eventually, they received venture capital funding, which reduced their shares in the firm to 20 percent each. After five years, the firm's revenues were such that it could make a public offering. This stock sale raised $20M, and the founders' 20 percent shares increased in value to at least $4M each. The founders got more out of their firm by giving up a portion of their equity to professional investors.

It is possible to achieve a "successful" venture financing deal, only to discover that you are not attaining your own personal goals. In Chapter 3 we suggested that you define exactly what you want to do with investors' funding. Factors such as cash, freedom to do a good job, challenge, prestige, power, a house, a certain kind of lifestyle, and other personal needs should be considered. If you are unfunded and become involved in a deal that restricts your personal freedom and weakens your control over the business, it may mean that your personal goals are not being met. If this happens, you will not put forth your best effort and both you and your firm will suffer.

You also may be tempted to take whatever funding you receive and use it, even if it's less than you need. After all, you may reason, you can always get more funding later. This is likely to lead to trouble. Therefore, make sure you have commitments for all the funding you need or that you deal with a strong venture firm that will help you obtain later rounds of funding. If you cannot get enough money for your needs, do not go ahead with the deal because, as your business plan should tell you, you will probably fail if you do not have the full amount.

The Founders' Share: What to Do with It

The EXUS Case Study in Chapter 3 shows a sample division of equity among the founders of a startup firm. That division resulted from a distribution of equity method commonly used in businesses. It is a passive method, however, because once the values are assigned, they are hard to change; furthermore, the assignment of equity does little to help the firm achieve its objectives.

Richard M. White describes several alternative methods by which the distribution of equity can serve as a motivational tool.* Briefly, they are as follows:

> *Seniority equity*—The amount of stock owned by each principal depends on his or her length of time with the firm.
>
> *Sweat equity*—The number of hours worked for the firm is compensated by a certain number of shares per hour.
>
> *Milestone equity*—Agreed-on amounts of stock are given to the founders and key personnel as specified milestones are achieved.

Milestone equity, originated by White and his firm, Business Solutions, Inc., appears to be a powerful tool for motivating company founders, key managers, and important technical personnel. However, it can result in a complicated equity structure.

CASE STUDY: Everlasting Computer Company

If you don't need it, don't ask for it. The principals in the three-year-old Everlasting Computer Company (a fictional name) came up with a product idea that "would take the industry by storm." They believed that investment funds would allow them to implement a marketing program needed to launch this powerful new product. The company's business plan, which did not include any funding amounts, showed the following financial projections:

($ thousands)					
Year	1	2	3	4	5
Revenue	784	1520	3200	7600	8900
Expense	831	1300	2400	6000	7300
Net	(47)	220	800	1600	1600

As the net figure for year 1 shows, the firm would need only $47,000 in funding to implement the plan. (The founders had prepared alternative

* *The Entrepreneur's Manual* (Chilton Books, 1977) pp. 108–125.

plans for funding calling for $831,000 and $911,000, respectively.) Upon being presented with the Everlasting business plan, a principal in a venture capital firm said rather icily, "Why are you showing me this plan? You don't *need* me for anything!"

Everlasting decided to use its own resources to implement the plan. To the founders' amazement, the product did *not* take the industry by storm. Someone had apparently told the firm to seek funding, but the founders did not realize that they could implement Everlasting's business plan on their own.

CASE STUDY: Precision Image Corporation

I can't believe they tried to get us to tell them everything. Precision Image Corporation makes wide plotters for the CAD/CAM, engineering, and mapmaking marketplaces. The firm employs 23 people and has headquarters in Redwood City, California. At the time of this writing, Precision Image is in its first year of business as a startup, with no sales revenue. It has received seed funding and first-round funding leading to completion of a prototype.

Gary N. Hughes, age 48, is president of the firm. He is the former president of Memorex Canada and of Benson, Inc., a manufacturer of electrostatic plotters. He and three associates identified the opportunity for a plotter. It was not a product that Benson was developing, so they decided to form a company around the product concept.

The three associates, the prospective Vice President of Engineering, Vice President of Manufacturing, and Vice President of Advanced Development began approaching venture capital firms for funding. After several rejections, they finally realized that their timing was not right, that the product was not designed, and that there was no leadership for their business.

Through a mutual acquaintance, the three men were referred to Crosspoint Venture Partners. According to Hughes, "They are one of the few firms that will invest in a plan in the early stages, before the team is complete, before there is a product specification. They put in labor or dollars to get it to where it can be brought to venture capital."

Hughes and his partners entered into an equity partnership agreement with Crosspoint. Under the agreement they were provided with a $1 million line of credit, from which they were allowed to draw $250,000 initially. If they met specified milestones within six months, they could draw more money. The milestone comprised the assembly of a management team, the completion of the business plan, and the completion of the machine specifications.

Within six months the men had completed the milestones and had used only $190,000 of the funds. With Crosspoint they began approaching venture capital firms. At the time of the funding, Crosspoint was to put up the balance of the $1 million. With that, they needed only another $1 million to complete the first-round funding.

Hughes and his partners circulated 36 copies of Precision Image's business plan. This took time and plenty of leg work. "You just can't mail in your plan and expect a response," Hughes said. "The venture capital people have such a flow through their office that they just won't listen." Finally, several firms became interested enough to begin due diligence studies. Of those studies, Hughes says, "One firm put together a file on our product, us, and the market that was twelve inches thick. They put a lot of work into those studies."

As the studies progressed, the venture capital firms indicated an interest. Hughes describes several phone calls he received: "They would call and say how interested they were. They said 'As soon as you have your first funds, we're right in there. Don't worry.' But no one wanted to be the first to commit. As soon as the first one said 'yes,' they all wanted in. They would call and say 'After all the work we put in, you *owe* it to us to let us in.' We only needed a million and a half more, and I had to cut it off. I could have had six million."

Sixty days after they started looking, they had obtained $2 million worth of new funding: $1.5 from Sequoia Capital and $0.5 from Southern California Ventures. The venture investors own 54 percent of the firm and the equity partnership was dissolved. The new firm had a solid beginning.

We asked Hughes what he would do differently if he were starting the process today. He responded, "I should have taken the $6 million. That first round of funding, you're driving a stake in the ground and saying, 'Here's what it's worth.' Any additional funding after that dilutes your share. I would have had to develop a business plan that demonstrated a greater cash requirement, but I should have taken all I could get at the beginning."

Hughes now looks for nondilutive funding when he can find it. For example, he went to Japan, looking for a local partner to help Precision Image enter the Japanese market. After screening several firms, he granted a manufacturing license to one of them. Now he has a source of nonequity funds, a Japanese firm to sell the product in Japan, and a partner with a vested interest in protecting Precision Image patents in that country.

We asked whether Hughes had encountered any nonprofessional conduct on the part of venture capital firms. "Oh yes," he said. "With one firm, we presented our plan to one of their bright young MBAs hired to screen them. We had a sophisticated marketing approach in the plan, and he didn't know what we were talking about. He rejected our plan without understanding it."

Hughes tells of another situation that was far worse than mere inexperience. "We were making a face-to-face presentation to a large, well-known venture capital firm. I won't use their name. We asked several times whether they had any dealings with our competitors, and didn't get a clear answer. When we asked again if they had funded a competitor, the answer came, 'Not in this technology.' I guess we didn't listen closely enough, and we proceeded with the presentation. Halfway through it, it slipped out that they were funding a firm we consider a direct competitor. There we were, telling them everything. We were mad. We folded up our papers and left." We asked how that could have been prevented. Hughes replied, "We should have asked 'Did you fund Firm A?' 'Did you fund Firm B?' and so on, until we covered all the firms we considered competitors. They probably wouldn't make a deliberate misstatement."

SHORT STORY: Item on the TV Evening News

We spoke with a company founder who was later, quite by accident, mentioned on the TV evening news. It seems that the reporters were poking fun at the great number of businesspeople looking for funding. They quoted some local venture capitalists and a money broker, who derisively described one particular man going from firm to firm "desperately looking for money." Although the reporter did not name this person, he gave enough information to allow any reasonably intelligent person to know who he was. It was extremely thoughtless and unprofessional for both the reporter and the broker to leak the embarrassing news item. Demand confidentiality from those with whom you speak.

CASE STUDY: The EXUS Corporation Business Plan, Continued

The Table of Contents, Executive Summary, and Financial Analysis sections of the EXUS Corporation business plan are presented here. We have included them as samples in order that you may complete the presentation of your plan.

EXUS PLAN (4): EXECUTIVE SUMMARY

CONTENTS

I. EXECUTIVE SUMMARY

The Corporation
Product Concept
The Market
Marketing Strategy
Sales Plan
Manufacturing
Management
Board of Directors
Financial Requirements
Financial Projections

THE CORPORATION

EXUS CORPORATION, hereafter referred to as EXUS, was incorporated under the laws of the state of California on December 10, 1982.

EXUS will design, develop, manufacture, and market a series of video interactive physical exercise programs, enabling home exercise to be done without tedium.

The principal executive offices of the Corporation are presently located at 1751 Fortune Drive, San Jose, California 95131. The Corporation's telephone number is (408) 942-8750.

PRODUCT CONCEPT

The product line will be oriented toward applications of state-of-the-art *computer software technology to physical fitness and health.*

EXUS will market a group of software and hardware products that are directed primarily at the *home exercise market.*

EXUS will use existing game consoles and personal computers to implement the products.

Success Ingredient

The products will be offered as *unique animated exercise systems* with creative graphics designed to encourage active user participation.

The initial products to be marketed have been developed and are ready for production.

THE MARKET

The world's focus on fitness and health, and the "look good" trend that emerged in the '70s and accelerated in the '80s serve as the foundation to accentuate the timely introduction of the EXUS product line.

Time magazine, May 30, 1983, reported,
"...one of the greatest growth industries for the rest of the century will be the broad field of health. Americans are living longer, and the children born during the baby-boom years (1946-64) are trying to guard their youth as they head toward middle age. Fitness is a health-related business that is notably prospering and likely to get considerably bigger. The fitness market will reach $35 BILLION DOLLARS this year, up from $30 billion just two years ago. This is bigger than the combined sales of Coca-Cola, Procter & Gamble, and Kodak."

The market for EXUS products is a combination of both the personal computer software and home video game markets. This combined market will exceed $6 billion in 1983.

The personal computer and game computer products are in the process of merging into a continuum of computer products, which are differentiated by features and cost. Keyboard options and larger memory characteristics are being added to former dedicated games consoles, and game-playing features are significant capabilities important to the sales of the low-end personal computer products.

John McNee, Gallup Research Vice-President, said, "More knowledgeable purchasers, who buy more expensive video cassette players and personal computers, *want all kinds of new things.*"

The home exercise market is characterized by:

a. Need to exercise
b. Bad weather exercise
c. Need to relieve the tedium of home exercise

The EXUS products fill these needs, and are, as stated previously, a combination of the personal computer and video games markets. With the addition of the exercise market share, these combined markets, applicable to EXUS, should exceed sales of $10 billion in 1983.

Competitive fitness and health software is unavailable currently at retail. Software has not been developed with the fitness and health-oriented consumer in mind.

MARKETING STRATEGY

The EXUS product line will take a unique place in the market, as animated exercise systems that physically interact users with computers, and be portrayed as a totally-new set of products.

Through design, performance, packaging, advertising and promotion, EXUS products will be positioned in the marketplace to present this new product category.

Aggressive product promotion and publicity will be employed to firmly establish EXUS in this category, aiming sharply for the Atari 2600VCS, 400, 800, and 1200 computers, which represent an installed base of 16.4 million units.

With slight modification of the EXUS software, at an approximate cost of $3000 per title, we can broaden our appeal to owners of Apple, IBM, and Commodore computers, which represent an additional 2,800,000 installed base.

Marketing energies will be concentrated on the target audience: fitness and health conscious families, both adults and children, and single men and women.

SALES PLAN

The products will be sold through major retail chains and appropriate distributors for other channels.

Initally, EXUS will conduct tests in 1983 on the "Jogger" video cartridge and "Foot Craz" activity platform. Northern California department store chains, bookstore chains, and computer store chains will participate in the test. Catalog houses and premium accounts will also be included in the initial marketing stage.

We expect to sell 36,000 units (cartridge and platform) at $40 to the trade for a 1983 sales total of $1.4 million.

During the balance of 1983, a sales strategy will be developed to include national and regional accounts, i.e.:

National—Sears, Montgomery Ward, JC Penney, K-Mart, Toys R Us
Regional—Venture, Target, Wal-Mart
Special Trade Classes—Department stores, record stores, drug chains, audio/video specialty stores, sporting goods stores, and discounters.

A national manufacturer's sales representative network will be appointed in 1983.

EXUS will develop retail direct pricing, dating, delivery, warehousing, and freight allowance policies.

In addition to the 1983 test phase, EXUS will identify and contact high visibility premium accounts through which software can be directly marketed—that is:

Direct Mail—American Express catalogs, mailers, and invoice stuffers
Direct Marketers—JS&A, Sharper Image
Direct Mail Syndicators—Chevron, Shell, Texaco, Bank of America
Anchor Premium Target Account—Mary Kay Cosmetics, Weight Watchers, Avon, Tupperware, Amway, Quaker Oats, Kellogg
Military Sales—Navy, Coast Guard, Marines, AAFES
Premium Distributors—Citadel, Global
Incentive Accounts—Maritz, E.F. McDonald, S & M

Premium sales representatives will be appointed to actively solicit this business, and EXUS will attend all related shows and conventions—i.e., Premium Show, NMRD, Comdec, and NCC.

FINANCIAL REQUIREMENTS

EXUS is seeking $3 million to finance product development, initial production, and merchandising of the Corporation's products.

The management and directors of EXUS have every intention of making a public offering of the EXUS stock as soon as it is deemed to be in the best interest of this stockholders. A significant percentage of the equity of the Corporation will be offered in exchange for the first round financing stated above.

FINANCIAL PROJECTIONS

EXUS sales will exceed $50 million in 1987:

(Add 000s)	1983	1984	1985	1986	1987
Net sales	1,440	8,300	18,000	30,000	50,000
Operating margin	720	4,150	9,000	15,000	25,000
SGA expense	650	3,000	5,600	9,100	15,000
Profit, Pretax	70	1,150	3,400	5,900	10,000
% sales	4.8	13.8	18.4	19.6	20.0

BUSINESS PLAN ASSUMPTIONS

1. Sales projections are based on the sale of only two titles—"Jogger" and "Stomp."
2. Cost is estimated at 50 percent of the wholesale sales price. This 2-to-1 ratio should be maintained by utilizing off-shore sources of manufacturing.
3. Research and development expenses are incorporated in the cost-of-goods-sold.

EXUS CORPORATION
PRO FORMA BALANCE SHEET
($000 s)

Assets as of:	7/1/83	12/31/83	12/31/84	12/31/85	12/31/86	12/31/87
Current Assets						
Cash & marketable securities	2,850	2,466	2,371	2,181	1,896	3,671
Inventory	0	470	820	1,320	3,170	4,520
Accounts receivable	0	264	924	3,024	5,524	10,524
Total current assets	2,850	3,200	4,115	6,525	10,590	18,715
Fixed Assets						
Laboratory & test equipment	50	50	50	100	125	150
Furniture & office equipment	50	50	125	175	250	350
Leasehold improvements	50	50	130	230	380	555
Gross value fixed assets	150	150	305	505	755	1,055
Less depreciation*	0	15	50	101	151	211
Net fixed assets	150	135	255	404	604	844
Other Assets						
Organization expense	20	20	20	20	20	20
Deposits & other prepaid expenses	5	10	15	25	35	45
Total other assets	25	30	35	45	55	65
Total assets	3,025	3,365	4,405	6,974	11,249	19,624
Liabilities & Net Worth						
Current Liabilities						
Accounts payable	0	350	450	1,444	3,879	9,234
Accrued expenses	10	23	76	135	225	375
Notes payable	0	0	0	0	0	0
Taxes payable	0	0	172	340	590	1,000
Total current liabilities	10	373	698	1,919	4,694	10,609
Long-term debt	0	0	0	0	0	0
Common stock (state value $1.00)	200	200	200	200	200	200
Paid-in surplus	2,815	2,815	2,815	2,815	2,815	2,815
Retained earnings	0	(23)	692	2,040	3,540	6,000
Total liabilities & net worth	3,025	3,365	4,405	6,974	11,249	19,624

*Depreciation based on estimated five-year life.

SALES FORECAST AND PRO FORMA INCOME STATEMENT
($000s)

	1983 (6 mos.)		1984				1985	1986	1987
	3rd. Qtr.	4th. Qtr.	1st. Qtr.	2nd. Qtr.	3rd. Qtr.	4th. Qtr.			
Sales revenue (Net, incl. 10% return allowance)	520	920	1,500	2,100	2,100	2,600	18,000	30,000	50,000
Less:Cost of goods sold (50% of Sales)	260	460	750	1,050	1,050	1,300	9,000	15,000	25,000
Operating margin	260	460	750	1,050	1,050	1,300	9,000	15,000	25,000
Less:Selling, general, & administrative expenses	260	390	560	770	800	870	5,600	9,100	15,000
Profit before tax	0	70	190	280	250	430	3,400	5,900	10,000
Provision for income taxes (40% x NPBT*, Excl. ITC**)	0	0	76	112	100	172	1,360	2,360	4,000
Net profit after tax	0	0	114	168	150	258	2,040	3,540	6,000

*Net Profit Before Tax
**Investment Tax Credit

CASH FLOW ANALYSIS
($000s)

	1983 (6 mos.)		1984				1985	1986	1987
	3rd Qtr.	4th Qtr.	1st. Qtr.	2nd Qtr.	3rd Qtr.	4th Qtr.			
Worksheet calculations									
Sales (net of returns)	520	920	1,500	2,100	2,100	2,600	18,000	30,000	50,000
Total collection	296	880	1,240	1,900	2,100	2,400	5,900	27,500	45,000
Purchases (50% next month sales)	640	550	850	1,050	1,100	1,500	9,500	16,850	26,350
Payments (2 month lag)**2	360	480	600	950	1,050	1,100	8,400	15,850	23,650
Cash Budget									
Receipts									
Collections	296	880	1,240	1,900	2,100	2,400	15,900	27,500	45,000
New investment capital	3,000	0	0	0	0	0	0	0	0
Total receipts	3,296	880	1,240	1,900	2,100	2,400	15,900	27,500	45,000
Payments									
Purchases (inventory)	360	480	600	950	1,050	1,100	8,400	15,850	23,650
SG&A³	260	390	560	770	800	870	5,600	9,100	15,000
R&D	65	15	30	30	40	40	200	250	300
Leasehold improvement	50	0	25	0	0	50	50	75	100
Fixed asset investment	1000	0	10	0	0	20	100	150	175
Taxes (income)⁴	0	0	70	190	280	250	1,360	2,360	4,000
Total payments	835	885	1,295	1,940	2,170	2,330	15,710	27,785	43,225
Net cash gain or loss	2,461	(5)	(55)	(40)	(70)	70	(190)	(285)	1,775
Beginning cash	10	2,471	2,466	2,411	2,371	2,301	2,371	2,181	1,896
Cumulative cash	2,471	2,466	2,411	2,371	2,301	2,371	2,181	1,896	3,671
Less: Desired minimum balance	50	50	50	50	50	50	50	50	50
Borrowing needed to maintain cash balance surplus cash	2,421	2,416	2,361	2,321	2,251	2,321	2,131	1,846	3,621

*Includes initial inventory of 10,000 units.
**²Includes cash payment for initial inventory.
³SG&A includes wages and salary, fringe benefits, interest expenses, advertising, sales expenses, and general and administrative expenses.
⁴Last Qtr. lag on payments.

SOURCE AND USE OF FUNDS STATEMENT
($000s)

	7/1/83–12/31/84		1/1/85–12/31/85		1/1/86–12/31/86		1/1/87–12/31/87	
	Source	Use	Source	Use	Source	Use	Source	Use
Cash	479		190		285			1,775
Inventory		820		500		1,850		1,350
Accounts receivable		924		2,100		2,500		5,000
Fixed assets		155		200		250		300
Depreciation	50		51				60	
Other assets		10		10	50	10		10
Accounts payable	450		994		2,435		5,355	
Accrued expenses	66		59		90		150	
Taxes payable	172		168		250		410	
Common stock								
Paid-in surplus								
Retained earnings	692		1,348		1,500		2,460	
	1,909	1,909	2,810	2,810	4,610	4,610	8,435	8,435

7

Putting the Plan Together

In this chapter, we will discuss the process of putting the business plan together, how to modify the plan to suit a particular audience, and the final physical form the plan should assume. We have tried to present this process in a way that will minimize your labor. Our suggested approach is to:

1. Gather your data before the plan is written
2. Write certain sections of the plan ahead of others
3. Insure that all needed information is included in the plan to minimize rewriting.

The audience for the business plan will determine its contents and the emphasis (or lack thereof) you will place on each section. If your business is being presented to a nontraditional audience—that is, to a prospect other than a venture capital firm, you should consider tailoring it to fit the audience according to the instructions we will provide here.

. The *physical* form of the plan is also important. In dealing with professional investment firms, you are asking total strangers to hand over (potentially) millions of dollars. The first impression created by the physical form of your plan will help determine whether or not the professional investor reads it.

Larry Mohr of Mohr Davidow Ventures told us: "We have no other guide to a venture but its business plan. We get many plans that don't even have names and addresses on them. Some have fancy covers that they don't need. In others, the Executive Summary is nothing but a rambling essay on God and motherhood."

Needless to say, you should avoid such flaws in your own plan. Mohr added, "And the plan doesn't have to be lengthy. Venture capitalists don't stand at the top of a staircase, throw a stack of plans down the stairs, and pick the one that slides the farthest.

"It is very likely that a business plan will be rejected. It has about one minute to make an impression. If it's complete, well done, and clear, we'll at least give it a listen—even if it's not the best business opportunity."

The first impression, based largely on the physical format of the plan that creates this impression, is very important.

Modifying the Plan to Fit the Audience

There are several possible audiences for your business plan, each with different motivations in assisting you and different information needs. Figure 7.1 provides a summary. Modifications to the standard business plan are discussed below.

Limited Partnerships

If you are having trouble getting through the screen at a professional investment firm and funding is what you need, a limited partnership may be an option. In this case, as with all funding, you will have to give up something. A limited partnership:

- You will have to pass along tax benefits and/or revenue opportunities to the partnership. The tax benefits can be in any form acceptable to the IRS; the revenue items can include such things as a share of the profits or product royalties.
- Your accountant and lawyer will have to be involved, costing you approximately $10,000 to $25,000 or more up front for the required work and fulfillment of legal obligations.
- You may also be required to assign certain product rights to the partnership.

The tax aspects of the venture will have to be described in the business plan, probably with a tax opinion obtained from a qualified attorney

Figure 7.1 Selecting an audience: motives and information needs.

The Audience	Motives	What it wants from the deal	What information it needs
Venture Capital firm, SBIC, individual investor	Profitable investment	Return on investment	Standard plan
Referral sources: accounting firms, law firms, financial planners	Aid to their clients and associates	Fees, chance of additional work	Standard plan
Funded companies	To help others	Satisfaction, credibility	Standard plan
Limited partnerships	Investment, tax advantages	Return on investment, lower taxes	Standard plan, tax emphasis, revenue potential
Your employer	Improve sales, market share, company value	Improved sales, market share, firm value, better image	Standard plan, less on founders, more on product, market
Current or potential customers	Get a good product that meets their needs	Lower price prestige, equity, impact on final product	Information on product, founders, customers fund needs
Companies with compatible products, suppliers, distributors	Complement their products, cut R&D costs	Increased sales, lower costs, better image	Information on product, founders, market, funding, or other needs

or a private letter ruling from the IRS. Revenue opportunities also will have to be spelled out clearly in the plan, together with a clear definition of the product and its market, along with the rest of a standard business plan.

Your Current Employer

Your current employer will be very interested in the positive impact that your product suggestion will have on an existing firm's reputation and customers. In this case, the business plan should emphasize market and product information. An employer will be interested in any negative impact the product might have on the firm's existing products and its finances and operation. Officers of the firm will be interested in the resources that must be committed if your idea is accepted as well as the resulting impact on existing commitments.

Potential Customers

Potential customers will be very interested in the product itself and its effect on them—for example:

- Whether they can have an impact on the product design
- Find out about the firm as well as the management and technical teams
- Possibility of a price reduction
- The kind of funding or other assistance you are looking for
- How much of their time will be required

Firms with Compatible Products

Firms with compatible products will want to know about your product and its potential impact on their sales and operations. They will want to know about the founders and management team, and the funding or other assistance you are looking for.

CASE STUDY: Average Audio Products, Inc.

A comprehensive set of instructions on approaching audiences other than professional investors is well beyond the scope of this book. Such a discussion would center on how to form alliances, strategic or otherwise, between organizations. The Average Audio Case Study illustrates how this process could take place.

Average Audio, a fictionalized company, manufactures and distributes major components for a home audio system, including amplifiers, tape decks, graphic equalizers, turntables, and speakers. Its equipment has always been known to be reliable and inexpensive, but the selection of products Average carried has not been current with the technology. In fact, the firm had a policy of waiting until a new type of equipment had caught the consumers' fancy before it would be added to the product line.

Another fictionalized company, Tiger Audio, was formed by two engineers with some new ideas about making a low-cost compact disk player. They had studied Average's product line and were convinced that that firm's compact disk player would be a good fit. Therefore, Tiger decided to approach Average with the idea.

Tiger prepared a detailed analysis of Average's products, plotting the products against the year in which they were offered. It traced the rate of growth of the market for each product and located each of Average's products on those plots. Tiger also prepared a market analysis showing that the demand for compact disk players was rising significantly faster than anyone had anticipated.

Tiger's founders telephoned Average's president, explained their idea, and asked to make a formal presentation to Average's executives. Their request was granted. During the presentation, Tiger made the point that, based on the timing that Average had taken with previous products, it was significantly late to offer a compact disk player in Average's product line.

After some discussion, Average agreed with Tiger's assessment of the market and its timing. Indeed, Average needed to offer a compact disk player as soon as possible. Anticipating such a response, Tiger offered to turn its head start in product design into an advantage to Average. Tiger, therefore, proposed that if Average would provide funding for prototype construction and testing, Tiger would agree to allow Average to market the product under the Average name. The firms agreed in concept, and the sales portion of the effort ended while the preparation of a detailed business plan began. The project required the approval of Average's directors, and the plan was to be presented to them.

A business plan containing the standard topics was prepared, with a few additions and changes in emphasis—namely:

The *market description* for compact disk players was written into the plan, including the discussion of product timing that Tiger had prepared.

The *product description* for the compact disk player was included, emphasizing the compatibility between this product and the family of products already offered by Average.

At Average's request, Tiger's founders provided photographs and biographies to be included in the plan. These materials were provided to introduce the principals of Tiger to Average's board of directors.

The relationship between Average and Tiger was defined in detail, including ownership of the product, marketing rights, patents, and trademarks, as well as the financial aspects of the pending deal.

The plan was submitted to Average. Final changes were negotiated and the final plan was sent to Average's directors for review.

In this case study, we have tried to show the dynamics of modifying a standard business plan for a specific audience. Note that the standard business plan served as the framework. Alterations applied to a specific deal and concerned topics that were generally agreed on as relevant by both parties.

The Physical Form of the Plan

In addition to the facts, you are trying to convey an *image* of you and your venture via the business plan. The reader should get an immediate feeling that the people who wrote the plan are thorough and *professional*. The *completeness* of the plan provides information on the ability of its authors to think through the entire funding process and the steps necessary for building a successful business. The *organization* and *clarity* of a business plan tell the reader about the ability of the plan's authors to think and to write. Its *neatness* speaks to the working habits of its creators.

These are the first things that the readers of a business plan will learn about its authors, whom they have probably never met. Do these things matter? Think about this as an answer: If someone who was not thorough, who could not think and could not write, and who was a sloppy worker wanted a million dollars of *your* money, would you give it to him?

"It seems unfair," one principal in a venture capital firm told us, "that the burden of writing a good plan in good English is placed on the entrepreneur. But the lack of the skills needed to put together a good plan will likely cause management problems later in the life of the venture."

The following are specific hints and suggestions for the final form of the plan.

- A personal computer (PC) can save you significant amounts of labor and time. Therefore, if at all possible, use a word processor both for your own convenience and for the neatness and consistency it can produce. There will be many rewrites, especially in the product description and Executive Summary. It will be beneficial to present the financial data on a PC spreadsheet.

- Use a clear, legible type font. Use letter quality print rather than dot matrix (draft) quality, as it is easier to read.
- Make sure that your company name or founders' names and addresses are on the plan. (See Larry Mohr's quote at the beginning of this chapter.)
- Write the Executive Summary and prepare the Table of Contents last, to ensure that they reflect the final form of your plan.
- Ensure that every major topic, every figure or chart, and every appendix is correctly included in the Table of Contents.
- Use graphic formats for market and financial data where possible, and include pictures of the product and of the founders. You should take every opportunity to present as visual a plan as possible.
- Ensure that there are no spelling, grammar, or math errors in the document.
- Leather-bound volumes, typesetting, offset printing, and expensive paper probably will not be assets to your business plan. Instead, provide clear, clean photocopies of it. Generate a fresh, letter-quality printout from the word processor using a new ribbon on the printer. Enclose the plan in simple, neat covers, such as clear plastic ones or oak tag folders. Any one of the quick binding methods available at copy stores will be acceptable. Appendices should be reproduced, bound, and covered in the same manner as the body of the plan.

Confidentiality

Your business plan has value. The product description and market and financial information would be very useful to your competitors, saving many hours and thousands of dollars required for gathering the same information. It also could give them some ideas they had not thought of before. In effect, your business plan in a competitor's hands might put you out of business before you even start.

Your treatment and handling of the plan should reflect its value to you and to your competitors. If you do not protect it, the people to whom you show it will not protect it either.

The separation of detailed product, marketing, and financial information described in the previous chapters can help in protecting the information in your business plan. We suggest keeping the technical details in the appendices. Then deliver these appendices in person directly to the person assigned to analyze them. Stay with the material to ensure that the plan is not copied.

When you select firms to which you will send a plan, ask for the names of other companies they have dealt with. Call those people and ask them about the treatment they received in order to anticipate what you might encounter. Ask specifically about any problems they may have had with confidentiality, ethics, or professionalism. Also inquire if the firm is dealing with any of your competitors.

When you are dealing with an audience other than the professional investor, a confidentiality agreement, or a nondisclosure agreement, is routine. In our experiences with this type of audience, other commercial firms have always offered to sign such an agreement without being asked. With the professional investors, however, it is another story. A venture capital firm will say, for example, that its lawyers advise against signing anything. In our opinion, this is less the advice of lawyers than a point of pride for the funder.

We recommend that you *always* ask for a nondisclosure agreement. if the firm will not grant one and you want to send your plan to that group, then state in the cover letter to your plan that you asked for an agreement but were denied.

When you mail your plan, send it by certified mail and ask for a return receipt. A few days later, you will receive a signed card that the person has at least received the package.

Do not send the business plan to a company on a mailing list. Instead, first send a brief letter, with the Executive Summary attached. Follow up by phone. If there is interest, arrange to send your plan to a specific person.

CASE STUDY: Keller High Tech, Ltd.

Keller High Tech, Limited, is located in Vinton, Iowa. The firm assembles fiber optic cables as well as military and commercial electronics gear. It also produces microcomputer application software. Keller now employs 20 people, grosses nearly a half-million dollars per year, and has been in business for five years.

The firm had been in business for one year when it was purchased by William H. Keller, the President. At first, he operated without a business plan and performed most of the management tasks himself. This eventually drew his wife into the business, and they both ran the firm for a year and a half. These were difficult years because a major customer moved from the area, significantly reducing the firm's revenue.

Refusing to go under, Keller worked hard to increase the customer base. Now, looking back, he says that the firm was undercapitalized by $30,000. To help ease the crisis in the short term, he and his wife took low salaries. In addition, he asked suppliers for a list of their independent sales representatives and called each of them—offering them a chance to represent his firm's products. Several agreed to do this. Finally, a partner with financial expertise invested in the firm. Thus, slowly, things started to turn around.

The end of this difficult period marked the next phase in Keller High Tech's growth. Certain changes had to be made:

1. Keller redefined his working activities into three additional jobs.
2. He promoted from within to help with the firm's management.
3. At about this time, his partner wanted to leave the firm, so he campaigned to raise the funding needed and was able to buy out his partner's share of the business.

As a first step toward funding, Keller wrote what he called a "company overview," which contained much of the same information found in a conventional business plan, including descriptions of:

Product, its function, and the quality maintained
Customer base, competition, advertising, a review of the market, and the network of sales representatives for the firm
Management, employees, and company's structure
Financial data of the firm for the past three years

He then defined the amount of money Keller High Tech needed and was determined to approach no more than 25 investors—the SEC limit—for the funds.

The next step was to approach Vinton Unlimited, a local group comprising Chamber of Commerce members and others with an interest in the growth of the town. After presenting his case, he developed a list of 25 potential investors from among the membership and then approached each of them. Keller discussed the material in the company overview and invited all the potential investors to a meeting.

At the meeting, Keller and his wife presented the company overview and opened the meeting up to any questions from the potential investors. To Keller's surprise, the group asked many more pointed questions than bankers did. They were interested in his firm, and were impressed by the confidence that he and his wife had that Keller High Tech would succeed. At the conclusion of the meeting, he set a deadline by which interested parties were to invest.

As the deadline neared, Keller called those who either had not responded or had said "no," which resulted in several more positive responses. As a result of this effort, Keller signed up 11 investors.

The only problem with this approach seemed to be that people who wanted to invest were inadvertently left out. Therefore, Keller keeps in touch with all investors and potential investors with news of current activities and planned projects requiring further investment.

Keller High Tech's current strategies include both internal and external factors. Externally, Keller has defined four separate product lines for the firm, and has decided that each should amount to only 25 percent of the firm's business. He is also developing an application software package that is based on an innovative approach to the management of information in the nursing home business. Internally, Keller plans for no more than 20 percent annual growth because this rate can be financed from the firm's profits.

Keller is disturbed by some aspects of the business culture: "There is a false assumption that everyone in business needs to fudge," he says. "If you are honest, you bring suspicion on yourself." He has also had trouble with greed. "One supplier set his prices so high that it would put us out of business," Keller said. "I asked him why he was trying to do that. Eventually, we agreed on a more favorable pricing structure."

He operates under a simple personal philosophy: "What can I do to make other companies profitable? If I make them profitable, I'll make a profit as well."

8

Presenting the Plan

It takes 99 "no" answers to get to a "yes."

Old Sales Adage

In this chapter, we will discuss the process of presenting your business plan to your chosen audience. You will want to present the plan in such a way as to ensure that the plan gets to the people who should read it; that due diligence is performed ; and that, if the plan is rejected, you will have obtained readers' comments which you can use to analyze and improve the effort.

There are several audiences to whom you may be presenting a plan. The most popular and the most obvious, of course, is that of professional investors, such as venture capital firms, SBICs, and sophisticated individual investors. There are also referral sources, such as accounting and legal firms, financial advisors, and people who have been funded before, that can refer you to professional investors. If you are considering a limited partnership, there are accounting or legal firms that, for a fee, will help you with its implementation. Potential customers are another audience, as are other firms that may have an interest in your product because they see it as a complement to their own products.

In presenting a business plan, you will have several goals:

First, you must find the right person to talk to.
Second, you must understand the decision-making process that they
    will follow.
Third, you must win their attention and interest.
Finally, you must present, clearly and professionally, the opportunity
    that your business plan represents for them.

Getting Your Foot in the Door

In your pursuit to interest investors, other corporations, or even potential
customers in your business venture, you will learn what rejection is all
about. You may encounter people who ridicule you or your ideas, who
do not return phone messages, who do not keep appointments, or who
do not have the faintest idea of what you are talking about. Worst of all,
you will also run into an army of nice people who simply are incapable
of saying "no" when they mean it.

If you are not prepared for this experience, these contacts will waste
your time, sap your energy, and drain your spirit. If you have never tried
this sort of thing, it will help to understand a few facts about the process
before you get started.

Professional Investors

It is difficult to establish contact with venture capital firms, SBICs,
and individual investors. (See Chapter 4.) If you are not contacting these
potential funders through a referral, they will be polite, but your odds of
being funded by them are low.

In the larger firms, you will encounter a layer of people whose function is to screen out both you and your business plan. These people may
be relatively young and just out of school, possibly with their MBAs. In
some cases, they may be holding down their first jobs out of college and
their understanding of the "nitty-gritty" of business in general may be
low. If that is the case, their understanding of your plan will be somewhat
limited.

Not every junior staffer in typical firms is this way, of course, but we
have run into it often. During our interviews, company founders commented on this problem as well.

You will also find that the people in these firms tend to be very busy, especially the principals. Since the firms have ongoing investments which take up quite a bit of time, they may not return your phone calls. It will not be easy for you to make sure your plan is read, or to contact a principal for advice if it is rejected.

Potential Customers or Companies with Similar Products

If you are contacting a company with a similar product or a potential customer organization, you will probably make initial contact with someone the decision maker has placed in charge of screening contacts like yours. If you make phone contact and the firm does not know you, or if someone in the firm interprets your contact as a sales call, your phone calls may not be returned. For example, you may have conversations like this:

May I speak to Mr. Jones, please?
Mr. Jones is in a meeting. May I take a message?
I've left messages for the last three days. If I leave another, will he call me back?
I can't really say, sir.

If you address a letter to a principal in the firm along with some backup information, it will usually be routed to someone else. When you follow up, you may find that the person who did the routing does not remember where it was sent. The person who should have received it may deny ever seeing it and a typical response is, "It's here somewhere, but I can't seem to find it. Will you send me another copy?" Or you'll be told, "Your letter is interesting. We're reviewing it, but because of priorities, we won't be able to get to it until next year." When you finally talk with someone who *did* get and *did* read the material, he or she may say, "This is interesting. There are three or four other people in our firm who may be interested. Would you send letters to them, too?"

Thus, the process of contacting another firm can be time-consuming and tiring. If you allow it, it can go on for months. If you are new at it, you may allow yourself to be discouraged and perhaps even take the rejections personally.

The purpose of this discussion of negatives is to prepare you for dealing with thoughtlessness and rejection that may be encountered when you begin making your contacts.

Some Suggestions

Here are a few suggestions that may help. Some apply to all situations whereas some are useful only in specific cases. First, the general suggestions:

Find out who will make the decision. Usually you will be shunted first to someone who will *not* be able to help you. However, you will waste time and energy if you do not deal directly with the decision maker. It is all right if he or she later delegates someone else to handle the details, but always try to stay in touch with the key person.

Do not put up with rude or unprofessional treatment. If you feel that you that you are not being handled professionally, break off the dialogue. The unprofessional attitude you are experiencing may extend to other areas of the firm's business. If you do not feel comfortable working with the firm, take your business elsewhere.

Do not be discouraged by rejection. There is an old sales adage that says it takes 99 "nos" before you have a "yes." The same kind of math applies to your search for acceptance of your plan. Allow enough time to get through 99 negative answers. Many of the founders we interviewed had to approach a number of venture capital firms before they received funding. In one typical case, a firm backed by a solid referral sent out 36 copies of its business plan. Six of the firms receiving the plan performed due diligence studies, and three of them actually provided funding.

Note these specific suggestions for attracting attention and stimulating interest:

Get referrals before you approach professional investors. As we explained in Chapter 4, your chances of being funded are slim if you approach professional investors directly. Therefore, present your plan first to companies that have recently been funded and to the accounting and legal firms that represent them. A positive referral will greatly increase your chances of being noticed.

Get publicity if you can do so without giving away any secrets. Prepare news releases for local and trade papers. Write and deliver technical papers at appropriate trade conferences. These conferences are often observed by firms with interests in specific topics, and appearing at one may help you establish contacts. In any case, it will serve to build credibility for your firm or venture.

Attend a venture capital conference. Various organizations, such as the American Electronics Association, the larger public accounting firms and venture capital companies, and some universities hold periodic venture capital conferences that are attended by people from professional investment groups. Among the speakers are people presenting their business plans. The conferences tend to be expensive and there are some screening requirements; however, these events do provide an opportunity to present your business plan directly to an audience of professional investors.

Do your homework on the firms you contact. Never approach a firm without knowing at least the names of their key management personnel, the industry and product lines they deal in, and the key problems they face. Use this knowledge in your telephone calls and letters because they will be more inclined to respond if they think you are contacting them specifically rather than calling a name from a list.

Send a next-day-delivery letter to the president or CEO. Using this method, we have had our letters read and acted on by top executives in a matter of days. Call the office of the Chief Executive Officer (CEO) a day in advance and advise the executive secretary that a package will arrive the following day. Follow up the day after arrival by calling the CEO's office to find out how they plan to route and handle your letter and business plan. Your letter will receive prompt attention and you will learn the name of the key decision maker.

Please note: This method works well when the contents of the letter are appropriate for the top executive officer. Do not try to sell hardware, plumbing, or computer software this way. It is appropriate, however, for joint venture activity, formal participation in product development, and equity participation in your firm.

Send a good quality pocket-sized tape recorder. Include a tape containing a short message from you. The accompanying letter should say: "The recorder is yours. All we ask is that you listen to the message on the tape." This is an inexpensive approach compared to the cost of placing a salesman on a plane and paying for a hotel, rental car, and who knows how many drinks and dinners. A clever, attention-grabbing technique like this can be both effective and reasonable in cost if you choose your target audiences intelligently. We cannot recall who gave us this idea, but we do remember that it was described as as successful technique.

Try interactive testing. In Chapter 3 we briefly described this method of evaluating your management team. We asked several professional investors if they would participate in such a session. They said they would, if only out of curiosity. Such curiosity can work to your advantage, however, helping you gain their attention and understanding of your venture and your team.

Once you have succeeded in attracting the attention and interest of a particular audience, you must present your plan. Each audience for your business plan will have its own way of evaluating the opportunity you present, and each calls for a slightly different type of presentation.

Presenting Your Plan to Professional Investors

All professional investors—venture capital firms, SBICs, and sophisticated investors—will have similar ways of evaluating your plan. The steps they will follow, as described below, are called by some the *due diligence study*. The sequence and emphasis may change from one firm to another, but sooner or later, all steps are completed. This description combines the results of interviews with principals from several venture capital firms with materials from Richard M. White, Jr.'s book, *The Entrepreneur's Manual*, p. 166.

Initial Evaluation

Your plan will first be scanned or selectively read for only one to five minutes. During this scanning, several key questions are answered.

What does the Executive Summary say about the opportunity?
What is the management team like?
What is the product?
Is the marketing information complete? Is credible data on market size included?
Are the financial data complete?
How much money is needed?

One principal in a venture capital firm calls this the "slobber test," because it tells whether the plan was "slobbered together" or has substance.

The plan will pass this first step if it is complete, clear, and readable; if the product has intuitive value; if there is a clear difference between this opportunity and the competition; and if it deals with a product, industry, and investment level that the investment firm likes.

Face-to-Face Presentation:
Your Second Chance to Make a First Impression

Your first in-person meeting involves much more than a detailed presentation of your firm, your product, and your management team. Rather it is an exploratory session in which the investors begin to get to know you—how you think, how you solve problems, how you deal with others, and much more. They will ask questions that put pressure on you to see how you react. This audience will look for the following things:

- Your belief in yourself and in your product.
- Your credibility and integrity.

Before the session is over, they will have formed an impression of you—for better or for worse.

Your presentation should be well thought out, with reasonably professional visual aids and appropriate handouts. It should also be carefully rehearsed. Try to anticipate likely questions and have additional visuals ready to answer them. Use your judgment concerning how much effort you should put into the visuals. If you are presenting the plan to a small group and discussing only limited seed funding, transparencies created with a personal computer graphics program or transfer type will do. If you are presenting it to an audience of 500 people at a conference and looking for $10M, professionally prepared 35mm color slides or overhead transparencies are appropriate.

Your presentation leader should be able to deliver a stand-up talk professionally and to think quickly and clearly so as to answer questions without hesitation. Select the member of your team with the highest degree of these skills to give the presentation.

It is popular to say that your dress and appearance do not matter in a session like this. Some entrepreneurs take a certain pride in dressing casually, with a plastic liner full of pencils and pens in their shirt pocket. In California, it is popular to dress for the outdoors, as if ready to start jogging at any time. However, your attire and grooming are part of the impression you will be making on the audience.

Although there is no standard uniform that one must wear, some common-sense rules apply. For a man, a two- or three-piece suit, white shirt, dressy tie, and good shoes will do. A good sports jacket, slacks, white shirt, and tie are also appropriate. For a woman, a good business dress; a jacket, skirt, and blouse; or a two- or three-piece business suit will do. As of this writing, brightly colored sneakers are "in" for both men and women, but we suggest more conservative footwear.

For interesting reading on this and related topics, try one of John Molloy's books on business style and success. Molloy discusses the means by which people form impressions of other people, including clothing and grooming. As he acknowledges, judging others by their appearance could be called a game. You can choose to be offended and refuse to play. Or, as he suggests, you can learn to play the game to your benefit.

If you pass the presentation test, your business plan will be given a more detailed examination.

The Marketing Plan

The validity of your marketing information will be checked thoroughly. Some firms will assign a staffer to read relevant trade journals; pull information from the library; and make numerous calls to experts, customers, competitors, and suppliers—all to verify your market data. The ease with which your product can be sold will be reviewed, as will the potential distribution channels you describe.

The Management Team

Anticipate a thorough invasion of your privacy during this step. You and your associates will be thoroughly investigated. Before they are through, the professional investors may know you better than you know yourself.

Technical Research

If you have passed every test up to this point, the investors may hire professional consultants or engineers to check out your product. This is a good sign because once they start spending money on your business plan, you know they are seriously interested.

Financial Analysis

Every step in your financial analysis will be checked. Expense items will be torn apart and their justification assured. Revenue items will be tested for reasonableness and then probably reduced by a safety factor. Contingency funds will be included. The actual cash needed and its scheduling will be determined.

Negotiations

If you and your plan have survived the intensive scrutiny we have described, negotiations may begin in which the actual financial and equity package is constructed. If you have suggested a form for the deal in your plan, it may be totally ignored in favor of some other method of operating preferred by the investors.

Presenting Your Plan to Referral Sources

When seeking a referral to a professional investor from a law firm, accounting firm, or another funded company, the direct approach is best. Make contact by calling the firm and asking for either "the principal in charge of small business funding," or "the attorney who helped set up XYZ Company." If you are calling a funded company, ask for the President, CEO, or Chairman—whoever was the principal founder of the firm. You probably will not speak to him or her directly at first, but be prepared to do so. Some of the founders we contacted answer their own phones. State your case simply: "We need advice on preparing a business plan for the same venture capital firm that funded you. Would you be willing to help?" You will be surprised at how many are willing to come to your aid.

If the contacts you develop do not feel right or you are not handled properly, then drop the contact. In dealing with several firms, we began to develop very strange feelings. In one case, people from the firm overreacted; in others, they played ego games. In each case where these strange feelings developed, we learned later that there was something seriously wrong within the firm. One firm was running out of money; another was dealing with a seriously alcoholic founder; in a third one, the chairman was undergoing a distracting divorce. None of these firms was willing or able to help. If the contacts are strange, walk away.

Setting Up a Limited Partnership

Setting up a limited partnership with the help of a law firm and accountants will involve you with yet another kind of audience. In a sense, you are still dealing with professional investors, but medical doctors, lawyers, dentists, and other local business people may join in. This is more of an arm's length deal, however, and you are more in control of initiating the deal. In effect, you will be providing your business plan, disclosing just about everything even remotely connected with you and your venture, and offering a security. If the investors buy it, then you will have your money.

The presentations and evaluation process will depend entirely on the investors and the degree to which they feel they can trust you and the legal and accounting firms that have helped you put the package together.

Presenting Your Plan to Current or Potential Customers

Meetings with these contacts tend to be a little easier than those with professional investors. The people you contact will be, at first, more interested in your product than they are in you. After you have attracted the attention of the decision maker, a presentation will usually be scheduled with that person and several others, including a line manager or two and perhaps the people who would actually be using the product. If you are seeking significant advance payments or offering equity in the firm, someone from the finance department may also attend.

Your first task will be to sell the group on your product, the technical expertise of your team, and your ability to support the product after purchase. This is a straight sales presentation. If they like your product and are willing to buy, then bring up the issue of the investment opportunity. You might also ask them

To participate in a focus group

Whether the people who would use the product will help with the design to ensure that it will be of maximum benefit to them

To prepay the order to provide funding for product development

To sign a manufacturing license in exchange for an up-front payment and royalty

If you could use some of their critical equipment that you cannot afford, such as computers, laboratories, or machine tools.

If the potential customer is willing to agree to one or more of these arrangements, work out the details with an attorney. Ensure that you and the customer understand what each has to provide and what the result is expected to be. It is easy to get into trouble if your expectations and those of the customer are not the same. If, for example, you assume that the customer will pay for the product while the customer expects to get it for free, you have a problem.

Be very certain that the disposition of both equity in your firm and rights to your product are defined clearly. If a customer's personnel are involved in the design of a product and their capital equipment or facilities are used in its development, the customer executives might think they have an equity interest or some other rights in the product. Any agreements made should clearly define the expected result.

You can offer equity or not, as you choose. In the Davox Case Study discussed earlier, the firm first concluded a product sale with its customer and then reached a separate agreement for a share of the equity of the firm. In that case, investment funds were received in return for the equity.

Presenting Your Plan to Companies with Compatible Products, Suppliers, or Distributors

Firms that deal with similar or compatible products will probably also sell to the same customers you plan to reach. Therefore, your proposal can offer them an opportunity to expand their product line without heavy R & D expenditures.

As with potential customers, your first task will be to sell the group on your product, the technical expertise of your team, and your ability to support them once they have the product. They will also have to be convinced of the market potential for the product. A few suggestions follow.

- Be sure you have identified the decision maker and the process to be followed for making a decision. A regional sales representative may tell you that he or she controls the product line for the company. However, although these representatives normally have marketing input, the product line and marketing strategy will be set by one or two people at a headquarters location. Therefore, deal with the true decision maker, not a subordinate.
- Do sufficient homework on the firm to know its product lines, its basic customer set, its strengths and weaknesses, and how your product or proposal will fit into its operations.
- Arrange for a presentation before the decision maker at the firm's headquarters. Representatives of the firm may offer to travel to you, which is fine at the outset. However, sooner or later you will have to take your proposal to the firm's headquarters anyway. In our experience, the on-site presentation works best.

There are several types of assistance that a compatible firm can offer to you. For example it can:

Market and/or distribute your product
Participate in a focus group
Participate in product design to ensure that your product is compatible with its product line

Allow you to use critical equipment that you cannot otherwise afford
  such as computers, laboratories, or machine tools
Buy the marketing rights
Provide either debt or equity funding

If you are successful at selling yourself and your product idea, you
can open negotiations over which of these types of assistance are appropriate.

Be sure that you include a confidentiality, or nondisclosure, agreement in the dealings with the firm. You will literally be telling them
everything about your product ideas. The agreement should be made with
the firm and will be phrased somewhat as follows: "We'll take all reasonable steps to protect your product." The firm will not agree to guaran-
teeing the actions of its employees. Ensure that your agreement provides
that anyone working on the project or being told details of the project
has signed the confidentiality agreement. Then have each individual on
the project sign separate individual agreements on confidentiality. The
last thing you need is for one of the individuals on the project to see the
answer to a critical problem and start a new company using your ideas.

SHORT STORY: Presenting the Plan the Wrong Way

An entrepreneur seeking $1 million in funding to expand a jewelry
line met with investment companies and retailers whom he thought would
quickly see the merits of his idea. However, he became very discouraged
after seeking assistance for nearly two years. One consultant, who claimed
to know of investment bankers who might be interested, wanted $10,000
in exchange for writing a business plan and putting the founder in touch
with interested parties. After some haggling, the founder and the consultant agreed upon $5,000. The founder said that his firm did not have
the cash. However, since the consultant liked the product line of jewelry,
the founder provided jewelry with a retail value of $5,000 as payment.

An independent accounting firm agreed to review the business plan,
to contact interested parties, and to represent the founder to the investment community. However, first an audit was necessary. The founder
arranged for the accounting firm to audit the existing jewelry store location and operating records. All was documented and found to be in order,
at a cost of $12,000 to the founder. The accounting firm circulated the
plan to interested parties, but there were no interested parties.

At the writing of the book the founder is still seeking funding and
assistance to develop his project. He is now closer to where he intends to
take his business, but he has had numerous expenses along the way. Al-

though the accounting firm did help, it also got paid for the audit it performed.

The founder should have gone to one of the larger accounting firms, had the plan reviewed, and sought a referral. A discussion with noncompeting jewelry chains or other retail operations may have yielded names of investors who prefer retail operations.

SHORT STORY: The Case of the Bogus Broker

We met with a company founder who gave us a sad but interesting story on the condition that he not be identified. We will call him Pete.

Pete had tried several approaches to selling his business plan. Using a mailing list of venture capital firms, he selected some addresses and mailed out two dozen copies of his business plan. There were no responses.

He had approached several banks for a loan, but lacking sufficient collateral, he had been turned down.

Finally, Pete put an advertisement in the *Wall Street Journal*. He received several inquiries, including one from a person who said she had close connections with a European banker. After a brief telephone conversation, Pete was asked to bring his business plan to her office. He kept the appointment and described his plan and his problems in raising money. Pete was delighted when she said her banker was interested in the plan and would probably provide funding. As soon as Pete paid a $25,000 up-front fee, she could get things going.

Pete asked that the fee be paid from funding received, since the venture had no extra cash. The broker said that would be impossible and there was nothing Pete could do to persuade her. She wanted the fee in advance. Fortunately, Pete saw what was going on and escaped without losing his shirt.

Most reputable money brokers will work on a contingency basis. If you run into one who demands an advance fee, we suggest that you check him or her thoroughly. Ask for the names of companies this person(s) has found funding for and check to make sure that he or she is not a front. Check with the Better Business Bureau, obtain banking references, and even contact the attorney general's office in your county and the county in which the broker operates.

SHORT STORY: He Made the Earth (or at Least the Bankers) Move

Bob, a young but senior engineer, worked for a long-established medium-sized company that made seismometers—instruments that measure the intensity of earthquakes. Bob and two other engineers wanted to develop related products for an international market, so they decided to form a new company.

Bob was selected by the others to seek seed funding for development because he had the executive level skills of writing and talking with new people. The other two people elected to stay in technical research roles.

Bob attended local seminars where he told interested listeners about his plans for the company and the company's funding requirements. After 18 months, Bob got a recently formed local business bank interested in his project. He had some equipment collateral to back a loan, and the bank granted the loan and participated in the management of the startup.

Bob also got the older company to put up some funds toward his new firm's research efforts. A management consulting company offered to assist in preparing a business plan, but Bob felt it was not needed because the bank was already beginning to respond.

There were times when Bob was really worn out from the process of seeking funding and "doing all the talking." The experience highlights an important point, however. Bob was successful in obtaining funding because he was able to communicate the goals of the new firm, its products, and the founders' plans and needs. Without those skills, the startup would never have succeeded. If you or your co-founders do not have such skills, then send someone to a seminar dealing with this topic or hire someone to help you.

9

Evaluating the Result

By this time, you have probably developed a business plan and submitted it to one or more chosen audiences. If you were successful, you should be negotiating terms and signing contracts, and you do not need this chapter. If you were unsuccessful, however, this chapter will help you determine what to do next.

The failure of a business plan can drain the time, money, and spirit of its authors, and it may make you feel rejected or discouraged. What do you do next? Do you quit and go back to your regular job? Or, do you review your effort, find its weaknesses, and try again? Our suggestion is, of course, that you try again as long as it is reasonable to do so.

In this chapter, we will present a series of steps to guide your after-the-fact analysis of the business planning effort. This analysis will help you pinpoint weaknesses in the plan in terms of the chosen audience. When the analysis is completed, you should be able to decide whether you should revise the plan, select another audience, or drop the effort altogether.

Find Out Why It Was Rejected. Contact the people who reviewed and rejected your plan, and ask them for a brief explanation of their reasons for not accepting it. This may take some persistence because at this point there is nothing in it for them. If your contacts were with a staffer, ask to speak with the principal who made the decision. These are the kind of responses you might expect:

"The plan was not written well. It couldn't be understood."

"The plan wasn't complete. One or more critical items were missing."

"The plan wasn't credible. Insufficient supporting data were provided. The data provided were not believed."

"The management team was inadequate."

"The market is too small or is not real."

"The product and/or industry didn't interest the firm."

"The financial analysis was poor."

"Operational plans were incomplete."

As you get these and other reactions, delve further for as much specific information as you can get. In some cases, the answers can lead directly to corrective action:

If the plan is unreadable, rewrite it and resubmit it.

If the plan is incomplete, include the missing information and resubmit it.

If the management team is weak, find additional team members who can provide the additional skills and resubmit the plan.

If the financial analysis is poor, correct it and resubmit the plan.

The first three steps below are concerned with the gathering of information about why your plan did not succeed.

1. *Determine whether you should resubmit the plan.* Occasionally, you will run into someone who gives you one reason after another why the plan is inadequate and who says that no correction can make it acceptable. In this case, you are probably not being dealt with openly. Your contacts may say, for example, that the plan is not written well when, in reality, they do not like your management team and would not accept even a masterfully written plan from them. Always get the real answer if you can. If you do not have a clear answer, move on to another audience and avoid wasting yours and their time.

2. *Identify serious problems with the venture.* We suggest that you take the following kinds of readers' comments seriously:

"There is too small a market for your product."

"The product itself isn't quite right."

"The product cannot be successfully marketed."

"The management team is inadequate."

"You aren't asking for enough money."

Get a second opinion if you have not already obtained one and identify corrective actions that can be taken, if any.

3. *Identify alternative audiences.* You may have approached venture capital firms at a time when your particular product or industry was unpopular among professional investors. They simply will not invest in your particular product or business venture.

You may be able to find another audience, however, such as your customers or other firms with compatible products. Identify alternative audiences and the specific type of relationship you would need, tailor the plan to the needs of those people, audience, and submit it to them.

After gathering information, you have to determine what your next steps will be regarding your business venture.

4. *Determine whether you can make a simple change and resubmit the plan.* If you discover that changes in the plan will be accepted and that such changes are reasonable to make, then make them and resubmit the plan. These alterations may include editing and rewriting as necessary, providing missing information, and correcting errors in data or computations.

5. *Determine whether the planning effort should be continued.* If there are serious problems with your project, you must decide whether to continue seeking funding. Serious problems include the following:

Poorly defined or nonexistent market
Wrong product
Missing skills on the management team
Inadequate financing
Presentation to the wrong audience

These problems can be solved, of course. A new market definition can be prepared; the product can be redesigned; the management team can be strengthened; financing can be increased; and new audiences can be selected. As these changes are reflected in the business plan, the overall value of the venture as portrayed in the plan will be affected. Make some quick computations to decide whether the resulting venture will be worth a heavy revision to the business plan.

If you decide to continue the effort, then go back to the appropriate point in the business planning process and get to work. If you decide on a complete change in strategy, such as selection of another audience, you may want to go back to the beginning of the process and review each step in light of this decision.

If you decide to drop the effort, take some comfort in the fact that rejection and failure are common results of the process. Do you remember our earlier statistics? Only 1 out of 2500 unsolicited business plans is funded. Even with referrals, only 1 plan in 50 receives funding. So, you are not alone.

Your choices are simple. You may either go back to work at your 9 to 5 job or continue to seek out opportunities for new ventures.

Perseverance: How Much Is Too Much?

There are many books available that purport to teach how to achieve personal and professional success. Some are light, pop-psychology reading, whereas others are serious studies of how the human mind operates to create a successful person. Each presents a specific viewpoint or method of achieving success. However, certain common characteristics of successful individuals are mentioned again and again, including *self-confidence*, a belief in one's ability to achieve, and *perseverance*, the drive to achieve an objective in spite of obstacles.

These otherwise valuable characteristics, together with a belief in your product or service, can frequently cause you to spend too much time trying to make a business plan a success. That extra effort can cost you time and money. The obvious questions prevail: When should you keep trying and when should you give up?

This is a hard decision to make, especially if you are personally committed to your product idea. You created it, you see its potential, and it is hard to let that go. In this vein, Burak says, "You'll never convince a true entrepreneur that his or her product isn't saleable."

Our suggestion is to get some outside opinions from a respected business associate or a trusted friend. Both you and these persons should review your plan, the comments you have received, the alternative audiences, and the amount of work necessary to get the plan ready for resubmission or presentation to a new audience. If a detached third party feels that you should stop the effort, then give that recommendation some thought.

In our interview, we asked Burak for his view on when it was appropriate to stop and when to go on. He replied, "In determining how far to push a business plan, ask yourself these questions:

'Is the product or service proposed still viable?' 'Has enough time elapsed that the window of opportunity is closed?'
'How much time can you afford to invest?' 'Is more than that time needed to make the effort a success?'

"If you keep getting turned down, others who have never seen your plan may turn you down as well. There's an informal network that seems to operate, and news of an unfavorably received plan spreads quickly. There's not a lot of bravery in that group. Break out of that circle and assess other alternatives."

It is possible, though not probable, that you have a breakthrough product. The Haloid Company, in a well-known story, invented a unique process for copying printed materials. All the funding sources and companies they approached initially turned them down. Only later did they manage to get their "unsellable" product to the market—and the Xerox Corporation was born. Very few of these Xerox-type opportunities exist today—so few, in fact, that when a business plan claims no competition, many professional investors stop reading. From their viewpoint, *all* products have competitors.

CASE STUDY: Jiffy Lube International, Inc.

Jiffy Lube International, Inc., claims to be the largest 10-minute automotive oil change company in the business. In operation for six years, the firm employs 250 people system-wide and franchises 370 locations. Based in Baltimore, Maryland, the firm reports an annual revenue of $91 million.

W. J. (Jim) Hindman, the firm's Chairman and Chief Executive Officer, saw the need for a place where consumers could bring their automobiles for a quick oil change. "Six years ago," Hindman says, "the idea of making a living changing oil was not a reality. There were individual units around, but I saw a nationwide need. I wanted to build a company to change oil in 10 minutes, with the best service and the highest quality work in the time frame." Hindman proceeded to set up a franchise operation to meet his goals.

Hindman relied on trade literature to provide market research information such as basic financial and marketing analyses to launch the company. To raise startup capital, he sold $165,000 worth of stock and mortgaged his home for $25,000.

Hindman was not alone in thinking the business had a future. The Pennzoil company bought in with $1 million plus guarantees for real estate purchases. A few partners bought minority positions in the firm. Over time, other experienced executives joined the firm. In 1986, an executive vice president resigned from Tenneco and joined Jiffy Lube as its president.

Not everyone shared Hindman's enthusiasm, however. In the early years, he approached venture capital firms, but they were skeptical. "The concept was not proven," Hindman said. "They were looking for home runs, and the VC didn't think changing oil would do it. Our approach looked like a fad to them, not a lasting business. They looked at the management team we had then, and said we weren't a professionally managed company. They said we had no plan for succession. They just wouldn't listen."

On June 2, 1986, Jiffy Lube filed with the SEC for an initial public offering of 2,030,000 shares of stock.

"You have to have tenacity," Hindman declares. "We lost $5 million before we ever saw a profit. We made mistakes." Hindman and his team pushed by the losses and the unconvinced and forced his firm to be a success.

Jiffy Lube had a standard business plan prepared by an outside consulting firm with the participation of the management team. Ten-year financial models were used to prepare a five-year business plan.

Hindman has used performance incentives to speed the growth of the company and to reward those who contribute to its growth. His philosophy is based squarely on the free enterprise system. "I want my employees to own a piece of the company," he says. "Anyone who wants to purchase stock can do so. We have only one class of stock available to both management and employees. For senior management, we used a loan program. We gave them a loan, and forgave 20 percent of it each year for five years. For the rest of the employees, we have a stock or bonus program. One year, we defined a set of goals and objectives to meet, and every dollar we made over those goals we split 50–50 with the employees. The first year we tried it, we were $100,000 over our goals."

Hindman has also shifted emphasis in the planning and budgeting process. In a more usual approach, the annual budget is prepared and all operating plans must exist within its limits. However, at Jiffy Lube, the management team develops the year's plans and tells Hindman how much money the company will need. Jiffy Lube has grown much faster than anyone anticipated, but the need for more money prevailed. Hindman views it as his responsibility to go out and get whatever amount of money is needed.

Hindman's fundraising chores have not always been easy. In 1983, he had successfully worked out a construction loan with a Maryland savings and loan association. The firm was drawing $200,000 per week to keep up with its ambitious construction schedule for 61 franchise sites. In 1985, the State of Maryland closed the savings and loan, however, cutting off Jiffy Lube's source of funds. With little lead time, Hindman was faced with raising $1 million a month for six months. Company officers and franchises loaned the firm the first million; Pennzoil loaned the second; the firm's lawyer introduced Hindman to an individual who loaned another. So it went, until he met his goal at the end of six months.

We asked Hindman about any operational controls he used when he started out. He said, "If I knew then what I know now, there sure would have been some controls in place. I wasn't sophisticated enough a manager to know how important they were. We have controls now, however; expense controls, flash financial reports, and cash flow projections."

We asked what he would do differently if he were starting over. "I would have hired a top quality chief financial officer from the very beginning. We just weren't prepared to spend the money for a key financial person at the beginning. A good CFO makes a night-and-day difference in running the company."

CASE STUDY: Summa Four, Inc.

Summa Four, Inc., manufactures call accounting and digital switching hardware for the telecommunications industry. The call accounting product is used by hotels and others with an interest in recording the length and cost of phone calls and the number that was dialed. The digital switch application consists of both generalized hardware and software for a variety of end users, such as operating telephone companies and OEM manufacturers.

Headquartered in Manchester, New Hampshire, the firm employs 160 people and grosses $20 million annually.

Summa was started in 1977 by John Boatwright, who left the large telephone company environment with an idea. He felt that he could build an add-on device that would complement telephone company hardware by providing digital capabilities, such as call forwarding, that were not then available. Using his own money and an initial seed funding of $1.5 million from a venture capital firm, he started to implement his idea. In 1981, another infusion of capital was obtained from the original VC firm in the amount of $1.5 million.

Late in 1981 it became obvious to the founder and funders alike that something was going wrong with their strategy. They had not provided enough time and money to get through the long trial-and-decision cycle for major customers, so the board of directors decided to bring in a new management team.

Work on the turnaround began immediately. The new team's first task was to get an immediate infusion of cash to carry operations in the short term. An informal business plan was prepared and brought to the "insiders," the original VC firm that had previously provided the funding.

The new team convinced the funders that cash was needed, and $2 million was obtained.

The management team realized that a new product was needed to broaden Summa Four's customer base. Thus, the digital switch concept was developed. Over the next year, a formal business plan was developed, in which Summa Four's plans for the new product were spelled out. To develop the marketing section of the plan, current and potential customers were interviewed. In addition, information was obtained from outside marketing consultants. The marketing plan covered a five-year time period. The operational portion covered a three-year time period, including all elements of business operation and growth to be expected as a result of the new product implementation and the planned infusion of capital. The financial information in the plan included all business expenses anticipated over a three-year time frame, including engineering, marketing, and manufacturing needs.

Tight controls over the process were established, including goals and time deadlines for engineering projects, a financial and expense program outlining capital and expense timing and targets, and a detailed set of marketing goals and product introduction objectives.

Reporting was established, allowing effective communication within the firm and with its funders. Says Sam Occhipinti, Chief Financial Officer for Summa, "This reporting was critical. It allowed us to establish a strong, positive relationship with the VC firms. If we were not going to meet a milestone or a financial objective, we knew it in advance and were able to communicate that to the VC firms. There were no surprises, and they liked that."

The management team began a publicity program aimed at establishing a presence in the investor community and developing a following of potential investors who would be available when funds were needed. The firm began attending venture capital conferences sponsored by the American Electronics Association. At these sessions, representatives of firms make a six-to-eight minute presentation on the highlights of their firms and their firms' products. Interested investors sign up for more detailed presentations and a question-and-answer session in a private suite.

Late in 1983, Summa put on a full court press to interest potential investors in visiting their facilities and signing up as actual investors. In 1984 the original VC firms and three new firms committed to providing $4 million in funding.

With the committed funding, a formal business plan, and effective reporting and controls in place, the firm was on its way to a success. In 1985, Occhipinti was able to arrange a bank credit line of $6 million, which is now being used for operational activities as necessary.

We asked Occhipinti if he would agree with our assertion that a CFO is vital to a startup operation. He replied: "Establishing a presence with the investment community was a long, hard process. But building that presence and maintaining a dialogue with potential investors is very important. The task occupies a large portion of my time. The workload of keeping this communication going and completing a major funding effort would distract operational management and perhaps bring the firm to a halt. A separate financial officer can take on this burden effectively, allowing operational management to carry on with their business."

Summa is an excellent example of a turnaround in which a formal business plan played a certain role. Objectives and milestones were established, and a reporting system was implemented to identify expected problems. The result? A successful firm with the promise of a very bright future.

Conclusions

A great deal of work goes into the process of preparing and presenting a successful business plan.

If you are approaching the professional investment community, get one or more referrals. The additional advice you can get along the way will probably prove to be worthwhile, thereby improving your chances of success.

The path to funding is open only to the relatively few ventures that meet the immediate needs of the professional investment community. Even a good business plan can be rejected. If your initial approach has been blocked, try another. Continue to change your business plan, your venture, and the audience you approach until you succeed or decide that you cannot go on.

Do not depend on professional investors or anyone else for management skills your venture needs. To assure your own success, bring the best people you can find into the venture.

Include effective controls in the business plan both as a topic and as implemented procedures in the venture. Establish reporting procedures that keep all key personnel and investors informed about progress in terms of timeliness and cost.

With the approach we suggest, the keys to success will be in your own hands. If there is a way to make your venture a success, you can find it and make it work for you. If you follow this philosophy, there should be no such thing as an unsuccessful business plan!

Send Us Your Comments

We are interested in your comments on this book, especially any of constructive criticism. We are also interested in learning how you used this book. If you prepared a business plan using the ideas contained herein we would like to know the outcome—successful or otherwise. We may be able to work your suggestions into future versions of this material.

Please send all comments to the authors in care of:

Beta Enterprises, Inc.
P. O. Box 2747
Del Mar, CA 92014

Reference Reading List

The books listed below will prove helpful to you in learning more about specific topics within the business planning and venture management processes.

Raising Venture Capital

Raising Venture Capital: An Entrepreneur's Guidebook. Deloitte, Haskins & Sells, New York, N. Y., 1986.

Structuring the Business Plan and Running the New Venture

Richard M. White, Jr.. *The Entrepreneur's Manual.* Chilton Book Company, Radnor, Pennsylvania, 1977.

Personal Skills in Presenting the Business Plan

John T. Molloy. *Molloy's Live for Success.* Bantam Books, New York, N. Y., 1982.

Frank Snell. *How to Stand Up and Speak Well in Business.* Simon & Schuster, New York, N. Y., 1981.

Financial Management of the Venture

Ray H. Garrison. *Managerial Accounting.* 3rd ed., Business Publications, Inc., Plano, Texas, 1982.

J. Fred Weston and Eugene F. Brigham. *Managerial Finance*. 7th ed., Dreyden Press, Hinsdale, IL, 1981.

Marketing and Management of Marketing

Philip Kotler. *Marketing Management Analysis, Planning and Control*. 3rd ed., Prentice-Hall, Englewood Cliffs, N. J., 1976.

Setting Up Controls and Reporting for the Venture

Joseph A. Maciariello. *Management Control Systems*. Prentice Hall, Englewood Cliffs, N. J., 1984.

General Management

Peter F. Drucker. *Management: Tasks, Responsibilities, Practices*. Harper & Row, New York, N. Y., 1973.

Systematic Entrepreneurship— Finding the Next Opportunity

Peter F. Drucker. *Innovation and Entrepreneurship*. Harper & Row, New York, N. Y., 1986.

Appendix A
The Business Plan Process

The Process

If you have been following the sequence of steps presented in this book, you will do a significant amount of homework before writing a plan. This up-front investment in time can pay off either in an increased probability of getting assistance or in a valid decision to stop preparing the plan until additional information becomes available or critical factors change. In either case, you should end up with a more successful effort with less time wasted on rejected business plans.

How Much Time and Effort Are Required?

There are benefits in using the approach suggested on these pages. There is also some work to be done. At this point, the time and effort required to complete a successful business planning effort should be discussed.

In our interviews with founders whose firms had received funding, we were told that it takes a significant amount of time to put a business plan together. Typically, they describe their efforts as requiring from six to twelve months.

It is tempting to view the business planning process simplistically. That is, one should obtain an outline, sit down in front of a word processor and PC spread sheet, and crank out the plan in a matter of a few weeks. It is possible that business plans constructed this way have been funded. However, we suggest that you spend enough time on the project to ensure its success.

On the following pages, we have prepared a project plan to show how long such an effort might take. The result is illustrated in Figure A.1, which uses worst-case scenario and includes all the activities outlined in the book. We did not overlap any activities that could done in parallel with others. The time estimate for completing the tasks shown is about eight months.

We have allowed for long delays in the collection of market data and presentation of the completed plan. In addition, we have included holiday, vacation, and weekend time, as well as a small amount of sick time. We have also assumed that there are no outside factors to slow up the process. If you choose to attend a trade show, for example, to present your product and gauge customer interest, your plan will be very much influenced by the scheduling of that trade show. You may discover that the show you wish to attend does not have any additional room for vendor presentations, so you will have to wait until next year. Most significantly, we have assumed that the people preparing the plan have other responsibilities and must spend a considerable amount of time working to satisfy them.

Your business planning process may vary considerably from the one pictured here. Your methods of market analysis and market data collection may be different than ours; you may or may not use customer interviews. You may or may not use multiple outside readers to check your plan. You may use more than one person to write the plan and introduce overlap into the schedule. Keep in mind always that this plan should not be taken as inviolate, and adapt it to suit your needs.

Figure A.1 Business plan time line.

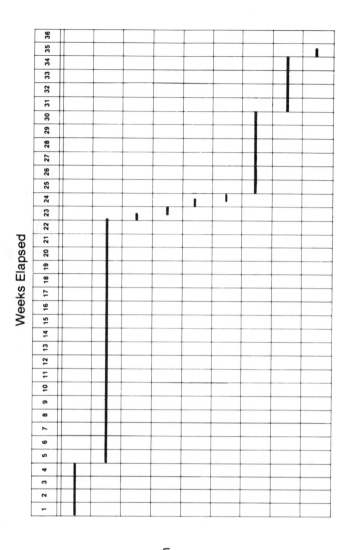

Weeks Elapsed

1. Prepare Product Definition

2. Prepare Market Description

3. Define Your Objectives

4. Analyze the Management Team

5. Analyze the Final Strategy

6. Assess the Fundamentals

7. Prepare the Business Plan

8. Present the Business Plan

9. Evaluate the Result

Business Plan Time Line

1. Prepare Product Description   **19 Days**
    Develop initial description   1 day
    Interview potential customers   3 days
    Brainstorming session #1   3 days
    Write product description   2 days
    Have laypersons evaluate product description for readability 7 days
    Revise product description   3 days

2. Prepare Market Description   **89 Days**
    Research trade journals   5 days
    Gather industry statistics   5 days
    Conduct customer interviews   10 days
    Brainstorming session #2   3 days
    Collect market data   50 days
    Brainstorming session #3   3 days
    Write market description   5 days
    Have laypersons evaluate market description for readability 5 days
    Revise market description   3 days

3. Define Your Objectives   **2 Days**
    What does the venture need?   1 day
    What do the founders want?   1 day

4. Analyze the Management Team   **4 Days**
    List management skills needed   1 day
    Inventory skills available   2 days
    Map available skills against those needed   ½ day
    Define management skills needed   ½ day

5. Analyze the Final Strategy   **3½ Days**
    Identify what you can do without outside help   1 day
    Identify what degree of outside help is needed   2 days
    Choose the audience for this version of the plan   ½ day

6. Assess the Fundamentals   **1½ Days**
    Review the product and the market   ½ day
    Review the founders and what is needed   ½ day
    Review the audience   ½ day

7. Prepare the Business Plan	30 Days
Prepare the financial analysis	5 days
Produce visuals for plan	5 days
Write and assemble final text	3 days
Have laypersons evaluate readability	5 days
Revise plan if needed	2 days
Duplicate and bind copies of plan	5 days
Produce visuals for presentation of plan	5 days
8. Present the Business Plan	**20 Days**
9. Evaluate the Result	**2 Days**

Appendix B
Sample Business Plan— Speech Plus, Inc.

We have provided this business plan as another example of a successful business planning effort. A. Keith Plant, President of Speech Plus Incorporated, gave us permission to reprint his company's plan, with the provision that certain confidential data be omitted. Also, the plan contained confidential research information from a market research firm, which has been omitted as well, as indicated in the Editor's Notes.

Executive Summary

Editor's Note: Certain confidential data throughout this plan have been eliminated. Missing data are shown by blank spaces in the text.

Introduction

Speech Plus, Incorporated, headquartered in Mountain View, California, is a pioneer in the commercial application of speech synthesis products. Prior to January 1, 1983, the company operated as Telesensory Speech Systems, a division of Telesensory Systems Incorporated (TSI).

Within TSI and as a separate company, Speech Plus has served the speech products market for more than eleven years.

Objectives

The Company's short-term objectives are to raise up to $3 million in new equity financing; to expand distribution and revenues; to accelerate research and development of new products and improve its leading technology for text-to-speech conversion; and to provide working capital. The Company's longer-term objectives are to increase revenues to over $ million per year by 1990, with after tax profitability exceeding %.

Business History of Speech Plus

In 1974, TSI produced the first commercial integrated circuit for speech synthesis. More than 300,000 of these circuits were sold. In 1982, Speech Plus, then a division of Telesensory Systems, Inc., introduced the first commercially acceptable text-to-voice converter, the "Prose 2000." More than 1,000 of these board-level products have been shipped around the world.

In 1984 the Company introduced the CallText family of products, which automatically converts any data base into voice and allows a user to access the information immediately by TouchTone (TM) telephone from anywhere in the world. The CallText system automatically answers incoming calls in voice, with user-supplied messages, and presents a programmed list of menu selections from which the caller may choose. The system prompts the caller to respond to the desired choices by pressing the appropriate TouchTone keys. The CallText system also initiates outgoing calls, transfers incoming calls in conjunction with a PBX, and communicates with external data bases via an RS232 interface.

CallText applications include remote order entry, sales and customer inquiry, dispatch, electronic mail delivered in voice, and banking and other financial services. For many applications using CallText products, the telephone completely replaces the computer terminal.

Major Accomplishments

The Company has achieved its premier position by virtue of its solid focus on management, technology, product, market, and financial leadership. Major accomplishments of the Company, resulting from that leadership, are as follows:

Management.   An experienced management team has been in place and working together smoothly since the Company was formed in 1982.

Improved Technology.   During 1984, the Company took aggressive actions to maintain its leadership position in speech quality by further improving its proprietary technology. As a result, the Company is now a market leader and is clearly positioned to participate in a growing opportunity to serve markets for products that incorporate text-to-speech conversion with telephony.

In less than one year, Speech Plus reached this goal. Tests conducted by the University of California, Berkeley, compared understandability of synthesized speech output produced by Speech Plus and a leading competitor. The results gave the Company an overall score of 91%, as compared with 86% for its competitor.

Product Family.   The Company has now established a product family ranging from board-level products through system-level products; it is the only major vendor currently offering a programmable text-to-speech conversion system. Such system-level products are installed in a variety of end-user growth market segments, such as telephone operating companies and other vertical end-user markets.

Competitive Advantage.   The Company's CallText products have secured a number of key competitive advantages:

- Leading voice intelligibility
- Highest pronunciation accuracy
- Good voice quality
- Programmability at the channel level, which eliminates any host programming requirement
- Emulation of any terminal to the host, providing compatibility with both SNA and ASCII environments
- Modularity and expandability
- Ease of installation

Vertical Market Installations.   The Company has penetrated and installed systems at key strategic end-user accounts in carefully selected priority vertical markets which the Company intends to serve vigorously in the future. These priority vertical markets include telephone operating companies, securities and brokerage services, banking, and insurance.

Licenses.   Technology licenses have been sold to certain key major manufacturers of computer-based workstations, including Wang, Texas Instruments, and a major computer manufacturer (to be announced later).

OEM.   The Company has established effective OEM relationships with several strategically positioned manufacturers. For example, Westinghouse Electric Corporation and Intel use the Company's text-to-speech board-level products in systems for manufacturing automation applications.

International.   The Company has created technology affiliations with leading international companies in order to quickly reach another fast growing market for the Company's technology and products.

Financial.   The Company has recently set new records for sales volume and sales backlog. This is a direct result of the 1984 actions to improve technology and the 1985 actions to expand distribution channels. Through the startup period, cash management has been the Company's highest financial priority.

Strategy

The Company's strategy for continued growth and leadership has five principal dimensions: Technology, Product, Markets, Sales and Marketing, and Manufacturing and Operations. Key elements are summarized below.

Technology.   Five major technology research and development projects are planned or already in progress. They include:

1. Further improvement of current synthesis-by-rules text-to-speech conversion technology, and implementation of foreign language capabilities in Spanish, French, German, and Italian
2. Investigation of software-only, and other lower cost approaches, in order to reach currently unserved market opportunities
3. Investigation of competing text-to-speech technologies, such as reconstruction technology, and implementation of appropriate new approaches in current technology
4. Investigation of Artificial Intelligence techniques to enhance quality and naturalness of speech output and input

5. Investigation of integration opportunities between speech synthesis and voice recognition, and between speech and vision

Product.   The company plans to expand its early sales lead in this industry by implementing three concurrent thrusts:

1. Aggressively pursuing the existing market for board-level products, primarily for OEMs applications
2. Actively selling technology licenses to selected strategic OEM such as Wang, Texas Instruments, and other major computer manufacturers
3. Developing a market for system-level and computer-peripheral-level products

Markets.   The Company's primary focus will continue to be on the commercial/office automation sector, with an emphasis on:

- Telephone operating companies, both as end-users and as resellers
- Large multi-site corporations with multi-geography networks
- Securities/brokerage service companies; banking and insurance firms

The Company's secondary market focus will be on the manufacturing/industrial and military/aerospace sectors. Historically, the Company has received a significant level of interest and orders from these sectors. The Company receives revenues from the Consumer/Handicapped market through its OEM relationships.

Sales and Marketing.   The Company has been very successful with a sales and marketing approach that skillfully weaves together vertical market specialists for direct sales, horizontal applications specialists to support the sales effort, and an OEM team for licensing and indirect sales. The Company plans to expand the size of the direct sales and distribution area in order to take advantage of expanding interest and order levels.

Manufacturing and Operations.   Manufacturing and assembly of board-level and peripheral-level products are almost entirely contracted out to various specialty shops in the immediate geographic area. The Company performs final quality control, burn-in, inspection, and shipping out of its facilities in Mountain View, California.

Management and Technology Team

The management team at Speech Plus is headed by A. Keith Plant, an executive with 24 years of significant experience in general management and marketing at IBM and Memorex. Officers of the Company have worked for such firms as Rand, Memorex, IBM, Acurex, and other industry leaders. The technology team at Speech Plus includes recognized industry leading experts with Ph.D. and Masters level degrees in the fields of linguistics, electronics, digital signal processing, and software development.

Market Projections

Industry Structure. Major opportunities exist for vendors to produce hardware and software products on several levels. Within the speech synthesis industry, the Company participates in all of them. They are:

- Board-level products
- Peripheral-level products
- System-level products
- Customized Synthesis Products
- Technology licenses, including software

Market Estimates. Table B.1, below, contains market projections, for all such hardware and software, for speech synthesis applications. It was prepared from data furnished to the Company by International Resource Development, Inc., a market research firm. These projections refer to factory shipments of synthesis hardware and software, and not the revenues from end-user products which incorporate the hardware and software.

Table B.1. Estimated Total Market Size for Voice Synthesis (Millions)

	1985	1987	1990	1995
Office/Commercial				
Manufacturing/Industrial				
Military/Aerospace				
Consumer/Handicapped				
Total Speech Synthesis Market	$100	$265	$705	$1,500

Editor's Note: These figures (and Table B.2) are confidential and have been deliberately omitted.
SOURCE: International Resource Development, Inc., Norwalk, Conn.

Market Analysis

Introduction

The decentralization of information processing during the 1960s enabled local, personal interaction on remote video display terminals. Advances during the 1970s added intelligence to those terminals, and by the 1980s the capabilities of 1960s computers were available on the desktop.

Today's computers are clearly among the most capable of tools; they perform arithmetic and logical operations at great speed and store and access voluminous amounts of information. However, until recently, they were all designed to communicate almost solely in the form of coded numbers and text, typically entered from a keyboard and displayed on a crt or printer.

Humans, on the other hand, generally prefer to communicate by using some form of natural language. If computers could be taught to both speak and listen, their value would increase significantly. The ordinary telephone could then assume many of the characteristics now reserved for the sophisticated /keyboard/screen terminal, and open up new application areas and services to many more end-users. This creates the explosive market for voice input/output devices.

Why Speech?

Speech is the most direct mode of communication we possess; thus, it is only natural to conceive of the ultimate man-machine interface as a spoken one.

No other sector of the computer and information industry dealing with input/output devices is growing as fast as the market for voice input/output. By 1987, voice I/O devices will show an annual growth rate of more than 50 percent, compared to a 15 percent growth rate for CRT display terminals and a 27 percent rate for workstations. Between 1987 and 1995, the voice I/O market will grow to exceed three billion dollars. (Source: IRD, op cit)

What Is Speech Synthesis?

Speech synthesis can be thought of as the production of speech electronically through the application of digital processing techniques. It may be based on digital recordings and play-back of actual human speech (so-called Stored Speech), or synthesis directly from ASCII text (so-called Text-To-Speech).

What Is Text-To-Speech?

Text-To-Speech converts ASCII text strings to speech, and can be implemented from a model of the vocal tract using sophisticated algorithms or rules (the approach used by the Company), or reconstructed from stored speech parts (not yet of commercially acceptable quality).

What Is Voice Recognition?

Voice recognition can be thought of as the process by which a machine can recognize and respond to a particular word or words. The majority of systems only recognize the input of speakers who have trained the system. Further developments should allow for systems that can recognize input from many speakers without training the system.

Compared with speech synthesis, voice recognition is a much more difficult technology, especially natural language voice input which would allow users to speak to their machines as easily and spontaneously as to other human beings. Numerous disciplines are involved, including pattern recognition, information theory, linguistics, artificial intelligence, and others; and progress to date has been slow.

Market Projections

All market projections are from the IRD report previously cited. Missing data are shown as $ and   % .

Total Market.   The total market size for manufacturer shipments of hardware and software, for voice synthesis and voice recognition together, has been forecast to grow from $115 million in 1985 to over $3.4 billion in 1995. This is shown below in Table B.3.

Table B.3. Total Market Size (Millions)

	1985	1987	1990	1995
Total Voice Synthesis	$100	$265	$ 705	$1,500
Total Voice Recognition	15	157	1,110	1,968
Total	$115	$422	$1,815	$3,468

Voice Synthesis. The total available market for voice synthesis only, within the voice synthesis/voice recognition market, is forecast to grow from $100 million in 1985 to $1.5 billion in 1995. The Company expects 1985 sales volume to be about $ million, or a   % penetration.

Total available market for voice synthesis only, by sector, is shown below in Table B.4.

Table B.4. Estimated Total Available Market
          Voice Synthesis Only (Millions)

	1985	1987	1990	1995
Office/Commercial				
Manufacturing/Industrial				
Military/Aerospace				
Consumer/Handicapped				
Total	$100	$265	$705	$1500

Editor's Note: Certain confidential data in this section on "Market Analysis" have been omitted.

Office/Commercial Sector. Table B.5. below contains additional detail on market projections for the Office/Commercial sector of the total available market for voice synthesis.

These projections refer to factory shipments of synthesis hardware and software, and not the revenues from end-user products which incorporate the hardware and software. Verify/Prompt refers to Data Entry Verification, Proofreading, and Training Systems. Voice Mail/VSF includes Telephone Management. Comparable data for the other market sectors was not provided in the IRD report.

Market Penetration. If total voice synthesis market penetration remains at   %, the Company would be expected to have sales volume of $ million in 1995. Increased market penetration to the   % level would allow the Company to reach $ million in 1990.

Increased penetration in the text-to-speech component of this market will come about through the focus on system-level products in the Office/Commercial sector, where the value-added is greater; through the vertical market application sales and marketing teams; and through increased sales of system-level products for OEMs in the Manufacturing/Industrial sector.

Table B.5. Office and Commercial Sector (Millions)

	1985	1987	1990	1995
Total Office/Commercial	39	111	310	650

Editor's Note: These categories and figures are confidential and have been deliberately omitted.

The Company intends to establish working relationships with key value added resellers (VARs) that serve chosen vertical markets. One VAR has already been chosen in the New York/New Jersey area, selling products for electronic mail applications.

Trends. As is the case with any new market, specific size and growth potential is frequently difficult to establish. However, a number of key trends are emerging:

- Speech synthesis had its first major thrust in toys and aids for the handicapped. It is increasingly appearing as an output option for consumer products, and voice output is currently used in computer-assisted training and warning/indicating applications in all markets.
- The largest untapped potential for speech synthesis applications is in telephone information retrieval systems, including inventory inquiry and update, order entry, dispatch electronic mail, and telephone information systems (Audiotext).
- The outlook for speech synthesis, in particular, is a function of development at the system level. Speech synthesis becomes increasingly viable within the context of specific applications and systems that enable remote callers to use ordinary telephones to retrieve appropriate data base information.
- Speech synthesis is currently leading voice recognition both in volume and rate of growth.
- The market projections for the total market for both voice input and voice output through 1987 are fairly consistent among the major market research firms (KBL, Creative Strategies, SRI-revised 6/84, Frost & Sullivan 10/80, and IRD 3/85) See "Speech Tech '85", p. 17.
- Integration of voice recognition and speech synthesis will make

voice processing as a whole more familiar, and hence more palatable to a broadly-based end-user community.

Competitive Analysis

Text-To-Speech Conversion Products

Table B.6 below summarizes some of the major competitors in the commercial text-to-speech conversion marketplace.

Table B.6. Competition

Company	Model	Form	Tech-nology	Com-mercial Quality
Ackerman Digital	Synthetalker	Board	FS	N
Digital Equipment	DECTalk	Periph	FS	Y
Don't Ask Computer	Automatic Mouth	Softw	N/A	N
First Byte, Inc.	Smooth Talker	Softw	N/A	N
Infovox AB	SA 201/PC	Board	FS	N/E
	SC2000	System	FS	N/E
Intex Micro	Intex Talker	Periph	FS	N
Micromint	Sweet Talker	Board	FS	N
Speech Plus	Prose 2000	Board	FS	Y
	CallText 5100	System	FS	Y
Street Electronics	Echo GP	Periph	LPC	N
Votrax	Personal Speech	Periph	FS	N
X-Com	Dicton III	Periph	LPC	N

FS: Formant synthesis—Simulation of the formants, or resonances of the vocal tract
LPC: Linear predictive coding—a mathematical representation of the vocal tract as acoustic tubes
N/A: Not applicable
N/E: "No" for the English language model

Stored Voice and Text-To-Speech Synthesizer Chips

Voice synthesis chips, generally used in stored speech products, are manufactured by several companies, including: Texas Instruments, Votrax, Silicon Systems, General Instrument, NEC, Hitachi, and others. The Votrax text-to-speech synthesizer chip had been the de facto standard for several years. Silicon Systems recently purchased rights to the Votrax chip.

Such chips, together with software, have been used to produce low cost, low quality text-to-speech converters. The chip business is not a major thrust for the Company; with low profit margins per chip, it is best left to those who can manufacture chips on a very large scale.

Board-Level Products

By board-level products we mean printed circuit boards that can be plugged into a computer. This represents one of the earliest thrusts of the Company; "Prose 2000" is a board level product, introduced in 1982 as the industry's first commercial quality text-to-speech converter.

The Company's boards are frequently incorporated into other manufacturer's systems: such as the Westinghouse "Series 100 Voice Data Entry" system for factory floor applications; and the Intel Corporation iSWS 090 Speech Transaction Generator. The Intel iSWS 090 integrates a "Prose 2000" board from the Company for speech synthesis, and an Intel iSBC 576 board for voice recognition.

Current manufacturers of board-level text-to-speech conversion systems include: Speech Plus, Ackerman Digital Systems, Infovox AB, Micromint, and others.

Adding credibility to the significant untapped potential for the Company's board-level products is the recent report that IBM has developed a board for the PC that will act as a modem, and will support voice and data transmission, voice messaging and speech synthesis conversion of text to speech. (PC Week, May 28, 1985)

Systems

By systems we mean a programmable, multi-channel peripheral subsystem. The CallText 5100 is such a system, and is the Company's major thrust into end-user markets. The CallText 5100 is the only programmable system-level text-to-speech product that can attach to any host computer and deliver data base information in voice over the telephone, without requiring changes to host software.

Peripherals

By peripheral we mean a device that attaches to a computer or another device, such as a terminal, has its own power, but is not independently programmable. Information to be spoken is formatted by the host computer and sent to the text-to-speech peripheral in sentence format. The CallText 5050 and DECTalk (TM) are such peripherals. The Company's peripherals are frequently incorporated into other manufacturers' products and services, through an expanding company OEM program.

Manufacturers of commercially acceptable peripheral-level text-to-speech conversion systems include: Speech Plus, and Digital Equipment Corp. (DECTalk).

Technology Licensing

The Company has pursued an aggressive program to license its technology to such end-user industry leaders as Texas Instruments, Wang, and one other license that will be announced later this year. This provides a royalty revenue stream, and important market and end-user feedback.

Software

By software we mean computer programs supplied on floppy disk, used in common computers. A popular example is the "Smooth Talker" product from First Byte, Inc. It uses a proprietary synthesis technique, involving software only, for which they have applied for patent protection. The product is compatible with Apple's MacIntosh, but lacks commercial quality.

Evaluation

Published results are now available from several evaluations of speech synthesis systems; and further reviews are underway.

Following a systematic evaluation of four text-to-speech conversion systems, the Speech Research Laboratory at Indiana University in Bloomington reports that average listeners can understand synthetic speech essentially as well as they can understand human speech.

At Michigan State University in East Lansing, researchers are investigating how intelligibility is affected by several different speech synthesis techniques, such as: pulse-code modulation (PCM), Linear Predictive Coding (LPC), and the more widely established Formant Synthesis (FS) which is used by the Company.

Two additional investigations have been reported in the official proceedings of "Speech Tech '85," comparing the Company's CallText V3.0 with DECTalk V1.8. Both tests show clear superiority for the Company's product.

Accuracy. Table B.7 below contains the results of the accuracy test. This is a measurement of the accuracy with which letter strings representing words are converted to phoneme strings with stress markers. It is measured by a trained technician who is expert in speech sounds and their written transcription.

Intelligibility. Table B.8 below contains the results of the intelligibility test. This is a measurement of the extent to which listeners hear the same words and phrases that were spoken. It is measured by having individuals listen to a set of directly produced or recorded spoken items, and indicating what they heard.

Table B.7. Pronunciation Accuracy

	CallText	DECTalk
30,000 words, Webster's Dictionary	81.3%	77.0%
360 US cities	82.8%	37.2%
50 world cities	94.0%	34.0%
1217 male/female first names	79.3	64.6%
3169 surnames	86.5%	70.0%

Table B.8. Intelligibility

	CallText	DECTalk
244 isolated words— Open response	91%	86%

Competitive Advantage

Based on these independent tests of the Company's products, and based on early market leadership, the Company has secured a number of competitive advantages:

- Leading voice intelligibility
- Highest pronunciation accuracy
- Good voice quality
- Programmability at the channel level
- Emulation of any terminal to the host
- Modularity and expandability

- Ease of installation
- Reliability exceeding 10,000 hours MTBF per channel

Product Plan

Introduction

The current and anticipated strategic direction of the Company is towards the greatest "value-added" sector of the industry where profit margins are the strongest. This means focusing on system-level products and software, while building upon the current base of board-level and peripheral-level products. Technology licenses will continue to provide an underlying base of royalty revenue to the Company.

Systems

The Company's system-level products are integrated, by large end-users and network service re-sellers, into a broad range of turnkey products. These are telephone oriented systems, that enable the access of any data base by phone. Speech Plus is the only company providing system-level text-to-speech products that enable data base information retrieval over the phone.

Examples of end-user integrators of the Company's system-level products include: General Telephone, AT&T, the U.S. Government—Patents and Trademarks office, and others.

Examples of network service re-sellers who have integrated the Company's system-level products include: GTE, GEISCO, CompuServe, UniNet, and Tymnet.

Current Products.   The Company's current product line in the system-level sector is called the CallText 5100 Multichannel Programmable System. Table B.9 below contains a high-level description of the CallText 5100 functions and features.

Future Directions.   The Company is designing a new board that will support two channels on the same board. The Company plans to use such a board to develop a system functionally equivalent to the CallText 5100, but supporting many more channels at a lower cost per channel.

Table B.9. CallText 5100 Multichannel Programmable System

- Support for up to five CallText 5000 Telephone/Voice modules
- Text-to-speech conversion for unlimited vocabulary
- All five channels (with the same or different applications) serviced simultaneously using multitasking software
- Incoming calls answered automatically with user-supplied greeting message
- Dedicated RS232 serial port for each telephone/voice channel or multiplexed over one RS232 port to host
- Call-handling procedures executed on CallText 5100
- Incoming DTMF signals received and decoded
- Capacity to initiate outgoing calls
- Call-transfer capability
- Software utilities and support tools
- Assembler and C languages supported
- System diagnostics (on-line testing)
- Traffic management statistics

Board-Level

The Company will continue to be one of the leading suppliers of board-level speech synthesis products. Most of these boards go to OEMs for integration into peripheral-level or turn-key synthesis products. Some third-party software houses are beginning to market software for such board-level products.

Current Products.   The Company's current board-level products are the Prose 2000, CallText 5000 telephone/voice channel, and the Speech 1000. These are described below in Table B.10.

Future Directions.   At the board level the Company will implement foreign languages as they become available.

Peripherals

These are stand-alone devices which interface with a host computer or communication network at one end, with a telephone or audio output at the other end. They may also endow other peripherals such as a desk-top terminal with speech output capabilities.

Table B.10. Board-Level Products

Prose 2000

- Multibus (TM) compatible
- RS232 serial port
- Single channel voice operation
- Serial ASCII English text converted to speech in real time
- On-board amplifier to directly drive a speaker

CallText 5000 Telephone/Voice Channel

- IBM PC/XT compatible bus interface
- Single-channel (telephone and voice) operation
- Serial ASCII English text converted to speech in real time
- Connection to the telephone network via a modular telephone jack
- Incoming calls answered automatically, outgoing calls dialed automatically
- On-board amplifier to drive a speaker directly
- RS232 serial port for external computer communications
- Callable I/O drivers provided (BASIC, C, and assembler)

Speech 1000

- Stored vocabulary board
- Multibus compatible
- RS232 interface
- Uses LPC technology
- Up to 6 minutes of stored speech
- Very high voice quality
- Certified for RF broadcast by the FCC

Current Products.   Current products at the peripheral level include the Prose 2020, CallText 5050, and the Speech 1020. High-level functions and features are summarized below in Table B.11.

Future Directions.   At the peripheral level, the Company will implement foreign languages as they become available.

Table B.11. Peripherals

Prose 2020
• RS232 peripheral for text-to-speech • Supports one channel • Same functionality as Prose 2000
CallText 5050
• RS232 peripheral • Supports up to four channels • Same functionality as Call Text 5000
Speech 1020
• RS232 peripheral • Same functionality as Speech 1000

Technology Licenses

Because of the Company's early lead, and on-going research and development in speech synthesis technologies, there will be an increasing demand by other companies and late market entrants to license the Company's technology. When it does not compromise the Company's strategic technological position to do so, the Company will continue to sell such licenses. Current licensees include such industry names as Wang, Texas Instruments, and one of the largest computer manufacturers.

Customized Synthesis Products

In certain license agreements, there is a need for the Company to customize its products. The Company performs this work under a professional services work-for-hire contract.

Applications

Through actual installations, work-for-hire contracts, and on-going customer liaison during the sales order process, the Company has developed considerable application expertise in several areas as the following examples illustrate. This application expertise frequently takes the form of application software expertise, for which there is an attractive and growing market (35% Compound Annual Growth Rate. Source: IDC). Examples of such expertise are shown below in Table B.12.

Table B.12. Application Expertise

Inventory Order Entry and Inquiry
General Telephone Company
U. S. Army
GEISCO/SYSCO

Data Base Inquiry by Telephone
Large International Bank (trading info)
Large Health Maintenance Organization (insurance)
New York Stock Exchange
U. S. Government—Patents and Trademarks

Public Electronic Mail
CompuServe
Tymnet
UniNet
Telenet

Private Electronic Mail
Cummins Engine
Citicorp
Large Life Insurance

Telephone Information Services (911/976)
AT & T
Illinois Bell

Development Plan

Figure B.1 illustrates the Company's 1985–1986 Product Development Plan.

Application Plan

Introduction

This business plan looks at four major market sectors for the Company's text-to-speech conversion products. Each one is discussed in the sections that follow.

Figure B.1 Product plan.

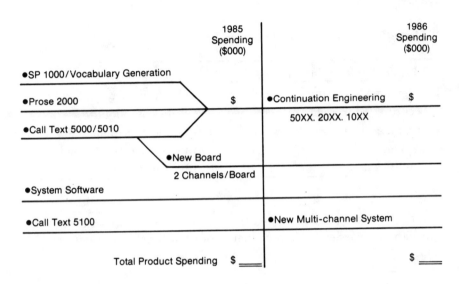

1. Commercial/Office Automation
2. Manufacturing/Industrial
3. Military/Aerospace
4. Consumer/Handicapped

Commercial/Office Automation Sector

This is the Company's primary business thrust, since it has the highest traditional voice-intensive and telephone-intensive communication volumes.

Within this market sector, the Company has prioritized those vertical market industries that have the greatest need for the Company's products and which will receive the greatest initial sales and marketing attention. Within the vertical market industries, the Company has prioritized those applications of the Company's products that have the greatest benefit to the customer, and thus have the greatest sales potential for the Company. These are summarized below in Table B.13.

Table B.13. Vertical Markets and Applications

Vertical Market Industries	*Applications*
1) Telephone operating companies	1) Order entry & inquiry
2) Securities/Brokerage services	2) Data base inquiry
3) Insurance	3) Public electronic mail
4) Banking	4) Private electronic mail
5) Hospitals and health care	5) Information services

Table B.14 below considers the vertical market industries and the applications together, yielding a matrix of prioritized opportunity for the Company.

Table B.14. Market/Application Matrix

	Telephone Operating Cos.	Securities/ Brokerage Services	Insurance	Banking	Hospitals
Order entry and inquiry	X	O	O	O	O
Data base inquiry	O	X	X	X	O
Public electronic mail	X	-	-	-	-
Private electronic mail	O	X	X	O	O
Information services	X	O	O	O	O

X = Currently Served by the Company
O = Near-term Sales Opportunities

Vertical Market Industries

Telephone Operating Companies. The highest priority for application development and market penetration is in the Telephone Operating Company industry; which includes not only the telephone operating companies as users of voice output products, but also as re-sellers of voice responses over their networks to their own customers; for example, GTE's California subsidiary, GTC, is a major customer of the Company.

This industry also includes the value added network (VAN) providers such as GEISCO, and Telenet; again, both as end-users and re-sellers.

The affinity of telephone operating companies to computer voice input/output is a natural one. This is especially urgent now that deregulation has opened up rapid restructuring of the industry and a scramble for new customers and new products and services.

Telephone operating companies will select new products and services using voice synthesis because: a) they are driven to reduce their internal operating costs, b) they need to find new customers, and c) they need to retain current customers by improving existing services.

The Company's speech synthesis products play a key role in all of these objectives:

- Speech synthesis is reducing operating costs by dispatching repair crews and handling customer service problems more efficiently
- Speech synthesis is being used to expand their revenue base by providing data base inquiry by telephone services, such as the various new "976" information telephone calls for which the customer pays a per-use fee
- Speech synthesis products are being used to improve customer service by automating and speeding up the directory information and service ordering functions
- Speech synthesis is reducing inventories by enabling employees to order parts from inventory, or from the vendor, over the phone

Financial Services.   Speech synthesis products are being used to deliver stock market quotations, "discrepancy on trade (DOT)" information, money market rates, and other financial data/news in voice as quickly as the information is available in the financial service provider's data base. Customers can receive a wide range of timely financial data by telephone, and can access summaries on selected stocks or place simple buy and sell orders directly. The Company's speech synthesis products are programmed to initiate phone calls to brokers or designated customers to advise them of significant events.

Insurance.   Insurance claims adjusters can input client accident loss information using a Touchtone telephone with a computer dialog at the host; sales staff can quote the latest insurance rates right in a customer's home or office; an updated insurance manual is always available to field sales personnel from any telephone; health insurance customers can even call for the latest information on their particular claim—all without costly human clerical intervention.

Banking.   Customers can inquire about account or loan payment balances, determine current deposit and loan interest rates, or automatically transfer funds from one account to another, 24 hours a day, from any ordinary telephone.

Hospitals and Health Care.   In most hospitals, nurses spend many hours looking at video display terminals in order to report patient lab test results to inquiring doctors. With the Company's speech synthesis products, physicians can use their TouchTone telephones to retrieve laboratory test results that have been fed directly into the hospital data base by automatic test equipment. Delivered in voice, these results allow doctors immediate access to critical data, and free nurses to perform patient care services.

Other.   Other industries that are candidates for speech synthesis products include:

- Transportation—reservations, ticketing, passenger information, fares, schedules, and real-time driver information
- Publishing—order entry, inventory inquiry, editing/production status, proofreading, telenews
- Education—student records/grades inquiry, class scheduling and registration, student/teacher appointments, and C.A.I. The Company's products are currently used to add voice output to an IBM personal computer based, self-paced C.A.I. system, called "Course Master"

In general, there is excellent potential for the Company's speech synthesis products wherever there is (a) a large data base with frequently changing data; (b) a large community of data users who need their information up-to-the-minute, and have limited or no access to computer terminals.

Applications

Order Entry and Inquiry.   The text-to-speech portion of this application involves reading back, for immediate verification, data base information (such as part name, price, quantity on hand or available), and verifying information keyed in from a TouchTone pad; and prompting of clerks performing order entry or inventory counts. Text-to-speech systems are also used for applications commonly known as "televoting."

Data Base Inquiry by Telephone. The text-to-speech portion of this application involves reading arbitrary, alpha-numeric text from a data base, and converting the information thus found into speech equivalent for transmission over a telephone to the inquiring person or persons.

Specific industry examples might include: field personnel receiving dispatching instructions, or order status, doctors retrieving patient care logs on the hospital floor, insureds retrieving a claim status, consumers retrieving fares and availability in a reservation system, bankers retrieving credit history or account status for a loan applicant, a stock broker retrieving a customer's trading history or unmatched orders; or a field service person retrieving dispatch and schedule orders via an ordinary telephone.

Electronic Mail and Messaging. This includes text-to-speech synthesis of messages and entire documents sent in ASCII code. Specific industry examples include: reading electronic mail to users that do not have access to terminals, or company procedures communicated to an insurance agent or banker in the field, or economic reports and out-trade information to a stock broker.

Telephone Information Systems. This includes the systems already widely implemented by telephone companies to supply directory assistance, but also includes any type of "911" prompting or "976" remote information retrieval.

Manufacturing/Industrial

This is the sector in which voice recognition has found an early niche; and there is strong potential in this market for integrated voice input/output systems—particularly for what are known collectively as "hands/eyes busy" applications.

The Company intends to give this market sector its next highest level priority. Through its OEM arrangement with Westinghouse, Intel, and others, the Company has enjoyed sizable orders for board-level and peripheral-level products that are integrated into manufacturing/industrial sector end-user products.

Examples of commercial/office automation sector products that are repackaged and sold to the manufacturing/industrial sector include: electronic mail of messages and documents to the factory floor, inquiries by telephone to inventory and production status—especially from field locations, and inquiry by telephone into dispatch and scheduling of maintenance and trouble shooting crews.

Military/Aerospace Sector

Prompting and warning systems, including "voice in the cockpit," are examples of major applications in this vertical market segment. In these applications, voice synthesis and voice recognition are obviously closely related, with turnkey and custom systems being developed by ITT, General Dynamics, Texas Instruments (a Company licensee), and others.

The Federal Aviation Administration uses stored speech in certain air traffic control applications. Speech Plus has supplied products for this purpose.

The military is also a major user of commercial/office automation systems. The Company is currently negotiating a very large order for one of the branches of the military service for system-level products, to be integrated by the customer into an advanced, inquiry-by-telephone based inventory control system.

Customer/Handicapped Sector

Applications for stored speech synthesis in this market sector include the following:

- Entertainment and Education
- Appliances
- Consumer Electronics Products
- Vehicle Warning Systems
- Home Security Systems
- Home Computer Applications
- Vending Machines
- Systems for the handicapped

Speech Plus serves the consumer/handicapped sector through its affiliate OEM arrangements. Kurzweil Computer Products, a division of Xerox Corporation, and TSI both offer products for the visually impaired market that use Speech Plus text-to-speech board-level products.

Financial Projections*

Assumptions

The following notes refer to the projected five-year financial plan that follows. Financial data through May, 1985 are actual. All other financial data are projected.

Accounts Receivable. Based on approximately 75 days sales in accounts receivable throughout the projected periods. Allowance for uncollectable accounts has been estimated at approximately   % of open receivables in the previous period.

Inventories. Based on Product Sales and Product Cost of Sales for four months in the future and taking into consideration the months of inventory currently on hand.

Prepaids. Based on a fixed monthly amount of $ being expensed with Prepaid balance remaining at $.

Property and Equipment. Based on a   % increase each year for purchases of Machinery and Equipment, Furniture and Fixtures, and Demo Equipment. Leasehold Improvements are based on a   % increase each year. Depreciation has been provided over a five-year life using the straight-line method.

Accounts Payable. Accounts Payable consists of inventory related liabilities and are assumed to be paid the following month.

Accrued Liabilities. Accrued Liabilities consist of all operating and administrative expenses and are paid one-half in the current month and the remainder in the following month.

Deferred Taxes Payable. Based on approximately   % of before tax income taking into consideration cumulative loss amounts.

Cost of Sales. Based on   % of revenues for Custom Software, Vocabulary, and License. Based on   % of revenues for Protocol Converters and   % of revenues for Product.

* **Editor's Note:** Certain confidential data in this section on "Financial Projections" have been omitted. Missing data are shown as $ or   %.

Operating and Administrative Expenses.   RD&E expenses decline to
    % of Revenue by 1987. G&A expenses are   % Of revenue
commencing in 1986.

Interest Income.   Based on   % of cash in the current period.

Financial Projections

The figures that follow contain financial projections for the 1985
through 1990 time period. They are organized as follows:

- *1985 Monthly*
- P&L
- Balance Sheet
- Cash Flow
- *1985–1987 Quarterly*
- P&L
- Balance Sheet
- Cash Flow
- *1985–1990 Annual*
- P&L
- Balance Sheet
- Cash Flow

Index